THE FIRST MILLION SABRAS

A Portrait of the Native-born Israelis

THE FIRST MILLION SABRAS

A Portrait of the Native-born Israelis

BY HERBERT RUSSCOL
AND MARGALIT BANAI

DODD, MEAD & COMPANY

NEW YORK

Library of Congress Catalog Card Number: 78-105295
Printed in the United States of America
by The Cornwall Press, Inc., Cornwall, N. Y.

This book is for our favorite sabras,
our children Yael and Michael

"And the Lord said unto Moses, I have seen this people, and behold, it is a stiff-necked people."

     *   *   *

"God would not have kept the Jews alive for so long, unless they still had a special role to play in the history of mankind."

—Diary of Theodor Herzl

Preface

It is notoriously difficult to generalize about a million in-
dividuals, which is what we propose to do in this study of the
native-born Israeli, nicknamed the sabra. We are not "Israeli
experts" by profession; rather, we live in Israel. Herbert
Russcol left America in 1948 and settled in Israel. Margalit
Banai, his wife and coauthor of this book, was born there and
is a sabra herself. What follows, then, are considerations of
the people we know intimately as friends, neighbors, relatives, colleagues, wartime comrades, and the man on the
overcrowded bus.

But after all these years we are wary of sweeping statements
about Israelis and their land. Such assessments are never quite
true. There are sabras who are perfectly happy on a desolate
kibbutz, and others who yearn for America. There are girls
who pop into bed as casually as the American fiction about
Israel would have you believe, and there are other girls who
served in the commando brigade called Palmach, lived for
years in a tent with boys and girls mixed together, and who
would have flattened you if you had so much as leered.

In sum, the sabras are people. And being Jews, they
are more contradictory than most other people. Still, sharp

traits have emerged that may be sketched; the traumatic events and peculiar pressures which have shaped Israel have also shaped the young Israeli.

He has come of age and has begun to mold Israel in a sabra image. And the questions arise: Who are the sabras and what is their make-up? How did they get the way they are? What do they want? Are they Jews, as we have always thought of Jews, or rather a new kind of eastern Mediterranean Semite?

The sabra is strikingly different from other Jews, and we are going to try to show how. The reasons are complicated, which is why good books about Israel are rare. They are hard to write. It is too much. The country and the life are too melodramtic. You cannot write knowledgeably about this place without pausing to take into account, and to explain clearly to the reader: life under the Turks before 1918; the British presence in Palestine from that date until 1948; the constant inflation; the Zionist idea; the complete impossibility of making long-range plans in Israel; the day-to-day danger, even though on the surface life seems tranquil; the claustrophobic borders; the ring of Arab countries that hate you; Hitler; the six million dead; the British opposition to Jewish immigration to Palestine; the three different Jewish underground movements at each other's jugular veins before 1948; the philosophy of the kibbutz movement; the Bible as both history and a practical guide to twentieth-century politics; three wars in nineteen years since the state was reborn, and four thousand years of Jewish survival.

All this is not merely the background for your story about people who live in Israel: it *is* the story of the people who live here. It all cries for a new Tolstoy, and he has not appeared. Or perhaps the only way to treat Israel is as epic, which the Bible does so eloquently.

Nevertheless, books about Israel hurl off the world's presses with astounding punctuality. In America there seems to be an entire subindustry devoted to explaining our nation and its citizens. Curiously, almost none of these books is written by an Israeli. We cannot tell you why this is so. Our own writers are prolific and they are all over the place, but the world for some reason prefers to learn about us from the professional Israel watchers.

It may be better to rely upon the views of foreign observers, but most of them are too sympathetic. Their hearts are in the right places and they love us too much to see us plain. They are blinded by their gallant cause. In all the books written about Israel by outsiders there are never whores or alcoholics or greedy bankers or black marketeers. There are only hero-farmers with a plow in one hand and a rifle in the other. We emerge from their pages rather like the cloth-dolls-of-Israel types which are sold in the souvenir shops of Jerusalem and Tel Aviv—here is the happy kibbutznik, the attractive girl soldier, the earlocked Jerusalemite, the quaint new immigrant from Yemen.

We shall try to focus sharply on the sabra, even if doing so jolts the popular misconceptions abroad of what we Israelis are like. Israel, of course, lives in constant danger from her enemies, but there is far more to us than the fund-raising glossy print of the dedicated frontier farmer with a plow and a rifle.

The sabra has kicked over the political chessboard of the Middle East. The Six Days' War brought our planet shudderingly close to the abyss of World War III; for that reason alone it is of the highest interest to learn all we can about him.

Contents

Part One ✡ THE SHAPING

OF THE SABRA

CHAPTER I

Profile of a New Breed: The Sabras

✡ "I have been pounding away for some time at a
work of tremendous magnitude."
—Diary of Theodor Herzl, 1895, author of
The Jewish State, and father of modern
Zionism.

The native-born Israeli has been given the sobriquet "sabra,"
after the wild cactus which flourishes in the arid soil of Israel. The fruit of this plant is prickly on the outside and soft
on the inside. This implies that our sabras are tough, brusque, inaccessible, and yet surprisingly gentle and sweet within. The nickname is given affectionately and is borne with
pride by our young, who enjoy the reputation that they cannot be "savored" from outward appearances.

The sabras are rapidly becoming the majority of the population of Israel. We in Israel are changing from a surge of
immigrant pioneers into an indigenous nation. A hundred
years ago there were less than 10,000 Jews in Palestine. But
in 1969 there were 2,400,000 Jews in the State of Israel, of
whom 1,075,000—nearly half—were sabras.

These figures sum up in a nutshell the Zionist adventure
and strikingly reveal that the sabras are taking over. They

have already begun to mold Israel in their own image, and that image is sharply different from the one of Jews in other lands. The sabras, the sons and daughters of immigrants from a hundred lands, are not merely another scattered fragment of world Jewry: they are New Jews. In their character and values lie the clues to Israel's make-up for the rest of this century.

The sabra was born here, and views the Middle East from within. He feels as much at home as does the reader of this book in his own native land. He feels a Semitic kinship with the Arabs and Arabic culture as no arrival from Odessa or Berlin ever could. Many sabras, including the outstanding sabra leaders Moshe Dayan and Yigal Allon, were brought up among Arab neighbors and speak fluent Arabic.

This, then, is the subject of our study: this still unsettled breed, this still inchoate genus (some say "ex-Jews"), the first million sabras.

*   *   *

"But you don't look Jewish!" is the dubious compliment a young Israeli usually receives when he goes abroad. The sabra is generally a head taller than his father, often blond and freckled, often blue-eyed and snub-nosed. He is cocky, robustly built, and likes to walk in open sandals in a free-swinging, lazy slouch. He speaks Hebrew either in a rapid-fire sputter, or in the singsong inflection that the Israeli writer Amnon Rubenstein calls "the arrogant, authentic drawl of the sabra." In a sense, he is a Hebrew-speaking WASP.

Roughly 40 per cent of the sabras are children of immigrants from Eastern Europe. Here, the boys tend to be angular, with abrupt gestures, and rather taciturn. The girls from this stock tend to retain the deep bosoms and comfortable hips of Jewish women in Slavic lands.

On the other hand, a full half of our Jews came from

Oriental and Levantine lands—Afghanistan, Yemen, Iraq, Iran, Egypt, Algiers, Morocco, and so on—and among these we find nut-brown lads and small-boned, tawny girls, who look much as Jews must have looked in biblical days.

The neurotic peculiarities of "the Jewish character" have melted away in the searing sun of Israel. If a team of enthusiastic and determined psychologists could transplant the sabras to the persecutions of the Polish and Moroccan ghettos wherein their fathers lived, all the "specially Jewish" traits would no doubt reappear within a generation or two. These racial traits are the effects of what Toynbee calls "the stimulus of penalizations," and in Israel these penalizations have been lifted.

As a result, the race has undergone an intriguing biological alteration. Eight months of sunshine a year instead of howling Russian winters; a diet of oranges and eggplant rather than herring and potatoes; a healthy outdoor life rather than the grubbing existence of a petty shopkeeper; a new-found idealism and political freedom—these make up the new mineral soil, so to say, that has produced that startling mutation of the desert, the sabra.

The best way to sketch the characteristics of our "new Jew" is to compare him with his father, the famous Zionist pioneer to Palestine.

The father was usually a devout Marxist as well as a devout Zionist; his son distrusts all "isms," beginning with these two. He was born and lives in Israel, period. The father gave lip service to believing that the Arabs were "just as good" as the Jews, but secretly felt superior to them; the son usually likes the Arabs, feels surprisingly little hatred for those who threaten him, and anxiously wants to come to terms with the Arabs somehow. The father, once he had reached The Land, rarely returned to Europe and he spurned travel as a waste of precious time better spent toiling in the desert; the son complains of cultural claustrophobia, travels abroads (especially to Paris) at the drop of a hat, and usually does not much like toiling in the desert.

Back in the ghetto, tailoring was as often as not the father's trade, and his father's before him; there is not one young apprentice tailor in Israel today. The average tailor is fifty years old, and the one sabra boy who *is* interested in the needle trade is studying haute couture in Paris.

Once arrived in Palestine, the father eagerly sought out the desert, and often a life of heroic self-denial on a kibbutz; the young Israeli of today is ready to die for the Negev desert, but he does not want to live there. By and large, he does not want to be a pioneer the way his father was. He much prefers to be an engineer, a poet, physicist, a film maker, a pop singer, or he thinks about opening a chain of hamburger stands.

The father is warm, gregarious, has "a Jewish heart"; the mother is "a Jewish mother"; the sons and daughters are usually emphatically unsentimental. The father often still counts in Yiddish, his mother tongue, no matter how dignified his calling, and delights in the corny Yiddish theaters that abound in Israel; his son understands little Yiddish, and detests it as the argot of the ghetto.

The father still reads Tolstoy or Schiller, or is often emotionally tied to Moscow and the October Revolution; his children are culturally attuned to the Beatles and Pete Seeger, and to the Paris of Sartre, Camus, and Jacques Brel. The father hardly ever drank—cossacks and storm troopers drank —but his sons and daughters have begun to sit in bars, wihch have sprung up to accommodate them. (Until a few years ago, a bar in Israel was a disreputable cellar frequented only by tourists and other questionable types.)

The father often had lost his entire family in a German concentration camp; the native-born son has never experienced anti-Semitism, and really cannot grasp it. The father usually had fled from Russia or Germany or from Arabic pogroms; the sabra never fled from anyone.

*　　　*　　　*

The sabra catapulted into world fame with his fighting spirit and sheer talent in the Six Days' War of 1967. Since then, he is the darling of the Western world, or the Prussian of the Middle East, depending upon your bias. The complete sabra, General Moshe Dayan, tough, arrogant, his own man, seems never out of the headlines, and we watch his every move.

Today, for most people abroad, the Israeli Army, which has been traditionally led by a sabra chief of staff since the state was born, is the symbol of what Israel is all about, rather than the Zionist slogans of the old-time pioneer in Israel. The wartime valor and tenacity of the sabra has created a new image of the Jew throughout the world; the sabra has cured to a remarkable degree that ancient social syndrome, Jewish self-hate. He is largely responsible for Jewishness being "in," at least in America. As Ben-Gurion put it, "Israel has straightened the backs of Jews everywhere."

Yet despite the sabra's militant reputation, the student riots that inflamed the world in 1968 and 1969 did not touch Israel. Ironically, no radical movement really excites our youth, whereas Jews abroad are in the vanguard of student riots, and historically Jews have always been among the leaders of social protest. The sabra does not rebel against the establishment, but rather identifies completely with his establishment's own fight for survival.* Only a handful of young Israelis have refused to join the Army because they

---

* When some American students at the Hebrew University in 1969 began smoking marijuana, it was the student body who warned them to cut it out, and who published a list of the offenders in the student magazine.

are conscientious objectors. The reason for all this is clear. The sabra is not searching for a cause, he has a very real cause: staying alive, defending his home, and building his new nation. With a sea of eighty million Arabs surrounding him and hating him, this is a full-time job.

Because his life is turbulent, unpredictable, and gravely hazardous, the sabra usually yearns for the delights of suburbia. It seems to him a blissful haven. He wants a cottage of his own, a little car, and vacations abroad now and then. His goal is the American glossy-magazine home with a washing machine and air conditioning and an outdoor grill—the whole sterile scene.

This fact has dismayed many young Americans who come to seek spiritual salvation in Israel, rather than seek it in the new communes of the young in New York or California. They behold the sabra entranced with his deepfreeze and his stereo rig, and they become disillusioned, and say that "the Israelis have become materialistic." But they miss the point: the sabra's life *is* rich and meaningful and spiritually rewarding; nevertheless, the sabra feels it would be pleasant to be physically comfortable and to have things as well.

Sometimes the sabra gets fed up with struggling—for the last half century riots, reprisals, border incidents, and open warfare with the Arabs have been the daily staple of life here —and he toys with the idea of emigrating. The siren call of America is heard in Tel Aviv as seductively as it is heard in Bagdad or Helsinki: in New York alone there is a floating population of at least forty thousand Israelis. Still, the sabra who lives abroad can never do so fullheartedly, as does, say, the Englishman who moves to America; the sabra feels guilt-ridden for abandoning Israel and will rarely admit that his absence from his country is more than temporary.

From May until November there is never rain in Israel, and the sabra lives every spare moment on the seashore and sets up puptents there with his family, or with his pals, his *chevra*. He is extremely clannish, feels a sense of common destiny with other sabras, and delights in the company and approval of his *chevra*. His basically hard and doggedly single-minded life makes him hypersensitive and intolerant of criticism—and unusually fond of other sabras.

He is passionate about soccer, archeology, and motorcycles, and often takes it for granted that people have involved love lives even after they are married. He usually considers himself a great lover, and rejoices in an open sexuality. He worries about Russian aid to the Arabs, and about the crushing income taxes which are a direct result of the Arabs always trying to bump him off. He worries about inflation, and a hectic economy, and the fact that *key money* for a three-room flat begins at $10,000. He worries, but not much, that the birthrate of the "Oriental" Jews (more than three times that of the Jews from Western lands) will make Israel a dark-skinned, "backward" people.

He is a devoted people-watcher, and invariably winds up an evening out by lounging in an open-air café, drinking expresso, chatting with his comrades, and watching the crowds and the girls in their miniskirts go by. He is devoted to his second-hand English-make car, and blithely parks it half up on the sidewalk, as there is usually no space on the street. (During the Six Days' War, as a gesture of national unity, the police ignored this forbidden practice.)

He is longing to take over political leadership of Israel, and curses the party-list system that enables the old-time leaders in their seventies to hang on in power until the grim reaper carts them off. He is quite daft about music, he can tell you the latest trends in off-off Broadway theater and in French avant-garde films, yet he is compelled at school to study hours of the Talmud and Jewish religious lore. He is an avid reader of American paperback books; *Time* magazine sells better in Israel than it does in France or in Italy. Israel has the highest per capita theater and cinema attendance in the world, and the sabra only now is getting television.

Having put his life on the firing line in the War of Independence in 1948, the Suez Campaign of 1956, and the Six Days' War of 1967—not to mention the "incidents" that go on month after month—he has little patience with grandiose and patriotic speeches.

He yawns when he hears hortative statements which begin "After 2000 years . . ." (a phrase, alas, much repeated in this book), and some sabras once facetiously proposed a club that would outlaw all solemn statements beginning with that unavoidable cliché.

It often shocks religious visitors to the Holy Land to learn that the young Israeli for the most part is nonreligious. The sabra, for example, usually resents the rabbis who ostensibly order his private life to an exasperating degree. As pork is forbidden, the sabra eats it defiantly under the guise of "white steaks," which are sold openly in stand-up outdoor restaurants. And yet, he loves the Bible passionately, and quotes it constantly in his conversation.

He is thoroughly bored with Jewish history *since* the Fall of Jerusalem, in the first century A.D., and is very excited about living now during the rebirth of the Jewish state; as one sabra put it, "Nothing happened for 2000 years, and now everything happens at once."

He feels himself proudly Hebrew and spreads his ancient Hebrew patrimony about him like a multicolored cloak, rather than as a shameful, half-hidden garment. He selects a splendiferous Hebrew name, and Goldberg becomes Har-Zahav. His newspapers, even the Communist, are dated 5729, from the Year of Creation according to the Jews, as well as the more prosaic 1969. He feels far closer to the ancient kings of Judea than he does to to his own grandfather.

Significantly, as he considers himself *Hebrew,* Israeli, he thinks of world Jewry and new immigrants as *Jewish.*

He feels much superior to the Jewish visitor from abroad who comes to Israel in ever-increasing numbers, and who is now the mainstay of the country's largest industry, tourism. It is comforting to know that they are intensely concerned with his welfare, and indeed often work tirelessly to help him, but he is aware that when the Arabs come over, it is the sabra's readiness to act and die that will determine whether or not Israel survives.

The sabra's complex feelings toward Jews abroad are colored by the fact that he can never grasp, although he knows the sad answers, why six million Jews let themselves be murdered by the Nazis. He never can understand why they did not die on their feet. This haunts him. It is a slur on his honor. It accounts for the one profound, centrifugal trait of the sabra: his readiness to act to defend his freedom. It has radically altered the Jewish conception of power and force; force was the Czar, who owned the Cossacks, who beat the Jews, therefore force was evil. For the sabra, the power of force has lost its evil nature, and the importance of this shift in Jewish mentality is difficult to exaggerate.

Thus, the sabra has decided, with his own guts, his own hands, his own wits, to shape the future of his nation (just don't tie his hands).* The belief that Israel exists by grace of American protection infuriates him. Israel will endure, he feels in his bones, if he has to live on potatoes and fight with Molotov cocktails. (Besides, this is the land of miracles.)

Such sentiment, of course, is common to freedom-loving people everywhere. It is schoolboy patriotism. In his leap

* In 1968, an Israeli newspaper polled its readers and asked them what the nation should do if, the next time, the Russians sent in their own planes and troops to fight alongside the Egyptians against Israel. Forty per cent of those polled said in that case we should take on the Russians, regardless of the consequences.

from the ghetto to the State of Israel, the sabra has landed with both feet in the nationalistic ninteenth century. But that is precisely the point: deprived of nationhood and a land of their own, the Jews for the last twenty centuries had nothing about which to be patriotic.

Three thousand years ago, the Hebrews of the Old Testament were resolute men and fierce fighters indeed, as well as great spiritual thinkers. In the first century A.D. the Romans captured Palestine, but only after years of grim and awesome battle with its Jewish defenders. Scattered to the corners of the earth, persecuted, shunted into ghettos, the Jews turned their vision inward. They lived out their lives apart in a ritual of prayer, abhorred force, and violence and pondered the workings of God.

But in Palestine, in our own century, Jews once again felt and acted as in ancient times. A young sabra once wrote:

Either we are facing our end or our rebirth. If it is our end, let us die like heroes. It is no people which allows itself to be strangled, and gives itself up to slaughter. A people is one which knows how to fight, and in time of need to attack. That is the kind of people I want us to be.

These flaming words were written by Absalom Feinberg, a leader of the sabra "Nili Spies" during World War I. They could well have been uttered nineteen centuries before by the beleaguered Jewish defenders of Masada.

CHAPTER II

The Need for Roots:
Masada and the Six Days' War

✡ "This earth Israel means something different to the Jews than Croatia means to the Croats, or America to the Americans. They are married to their countries; we are searching for a lost bride. We are homesick for a Canaan that was never truly ours. That is why we are always foremost in the race for Utopias and messianic revolutions, always chasing after a lost Paradise."

—Arthur Koestler

"The young Israeli has a religious veneration not for God, not even for Israel, but for the idea of the Jews possessing Israel. It is this concept which he worships, that he would defend with his whole being."

—Simon Raven

"The second time Masada will not fall!"

—Yitshak Lamden, Israeli poet

The sabra, then, is not something new under the sun. In a sense, he is three thousand years old. He is the Hebrew in his own land, reborn. He is the issue of a quixotic attempt to restore the Israelites who flourished for more than one thousand years, until Jerusalem was sacked by the Tenth Legion of Rome. The sabra has been hibernating in a kind of racial slumber since then, a folk memory of a nation that was.

There is little place for such romantic notions in the harsh realities of twentieth-century life. And yet the sabra, the most pragmatic of persons, accepts this "mythical" vision of himself quite matter-of-factly. For the sabra, the era of Jewish glory in biblical days is as the day before yesterday. After all, less than forty grandfathers separate the sabra who fought for Jerusalem in the war of 1967, and the Hebrew defenders of Jerusalem who grimly held out for four years against Imperial Rome.

The Romans were advancing everywhere. All that the Jews still held, apart from great Jerusalem, were a few scattered bastions. One was the City of Salt, where lived the mystic sect known to us as the Essenes, the people of the Dead Sea Scrolls. Another was the stark rock-fortress near the Dead Sea called Masada.

The year was 67 A.D. The fierce Jewish war against Roman oppression had broken out the year before. Riots flaring up had plunged both Palestine and Syria into turmoil. Cestius Gallus, the Roman governor, tried to put down the insurrection, but the Jewish Army smashed him outside Jerusalem's second Wall. He fled to the safety of the north, and the Jews hacked his Twelfth Legion to pieces at Beth-horon.

Rome took no chances in putting down the uprising that now inflamed Palestine. She hurled her full military might against the Jews. Nevertheless, in the first ruthless year of the war, the Jews almost won. This was a shock for the Empire. The situation was so grave that the Emperor Nero recalled his field commander, and replaced him with Rome's ablest commander, Vespasian.

Jewish hopes ran wild. The enemy this time was all-powerful Imperium Romanum herself, but there was a chance. They reminded each other of the stunning Jewish victory over an oppressor two centuries earlier. Then, in a bitter war that lasted twenty-one years, the Jews under Judas Maccabeus, "the Hammer," had shattered the Greek armies of Antiochus in 164 B.C. and had even recaptured Jerusalem.

There was a chance. It had happened before. This was the hope of the men within the walls of Masada, the impregnable desert stronghold.

*　　　　　*　　　　　*

Masada is a huge brown rock, with almost vertical sides, two and a half miles from the Dead Sea. Its plateau is a half mile across. It rises starkly, and unexpectedly, a sheer twelve hundred feet above the deep ravines of the desert floor.

There is a terrifying quality about this place that is caught in the awesome Hebrew phrase *Nora Hod,* which means "terrible grandeur." Travelers throughout history have been shaken by "this deep, this colossal ditch," "these deserts of vast eternity."

The harsh desert God Jehovah is real here. At the foot of Masada, it appears as though a wrathful, gigantic Hammer has smashed the boulders, ground them into rocks, then strewn them across the wadis. Sands are swept by searing desert winds, and the burning heat rises to 130 degrees. In the distance are dreamlike hills, lunar tablelands topped with craters and reefs like fangs.

Time means nothing. It is a dead, treeless universe. Mornings, the Dead Sea seems to befoul the air with salt and brimstone. One thinks of Lot's wife caught here, and of the steamy slime which Milton envisioned, in which Satan and his cohorts lay stricken and stunned after their apostasy. It is *Nora Hod.*

Masada means, quite simply, fortress. Here the detested Jewish King Herod had built himself a palace on the top of Masada. It was full of pseudo-Roman splendor, with mosaic floors, Greek columns, frescoes, Roman baths, and great storehouses filled with grain, dates, and jugs of oil and wine. The palace was built in a semicircle. The main entrance was through underground tunnels cut into the rock face. Slaves and mules carried water in jugs up to the cisterns on top, along the steep, treacherous train known to this day as "The Snake Path." Herod designed his palace at Masada to withstand a long siege. Besides being a sycophant to Roman emperors, he was paranoic and had murdered his wife and sons.

In 4 B.C. Herod died. Ten years later Masada became a small garrison for Roman soldiers. At the beginning of the Jewish war a force of Jews captured Masada and killed the legionnaires they found there. These Jews were a grim, desperate band, made up of Essenes, Zealots, and the tough desperados that the Romans called *Sicarii*, or Jewish dagger-men.

These Jews brought their wives and children to Masada (it was one day's journey from Jerusalem), and it was to be their home for the next seven years. They numbered almost a thousand people. They had come, as Josephus records, "to the fastness of Masada to defy the conqueror to the last."

The war dragged into its third year, and across Palestine the last Jewish strongholds still held out. Vespasian, the Roman supreme commander, had needed a full year of grim fighting to reduce the Jewish Army in Galilee, and he had still not taken the capital, Jerusalem. Attack after attack against the city failed to crush its defenders. The war ground to a standstill. Vespasian left for Rome, where he had just been acclaimed emperor, and his son Titus took over the task of seizing the defiant city.

Titus decided to risk an all-out attack. For two weeks, siege guns hurled rocks against Jerusalem's Northern Wall, tearing gaping holes in its ramparts. Through these holes the Romans streamed, and were met by the unyielding Jews. After fourteen days of savage combat—man against man, sword against sword—the Romans were forced to retreat.

Titus, his army bady cut, realized that he could not defeat the Jews of Jerusalem in open combat. He began a siege to starve them into submission. It was one of the great sieges of antiquity, spoken of with awe even by Roman historians. Titus was compelled to bring in 80,000 troops against the 23,400 Jewish defenders. This was a staggering army—Alexander the Great had used only 32,000 men to carve his empire.

Within Jerusalem thousands died of pestilence and starvation. The city became a nightmare. Leaving its gates was forbidden upon pain of death. Discipline was excellent, however; those Jews who protested against holding out were simply tossed by Zealots over the city wall.

Titus ordered the construction of an earthen wall as high as the wall around Jerusalem itself. With this new outer wall, he sealed off the city. It was now impossible for food and water to reach the defenders within. Any Jew caught trying to forage food outside the wall was crucified by the Romans on top of the new wall. The historian Josephus records that sometimes five hundred starving Jews a day thus died. The air was vile with the stench of rotting flesh, and the agonized screams of the crucified never ceased. Yet the Jews still would not abandon Jerusalem. They held out for another bitter year—the fourth year of the war.

But the end was inevitable. Four terrible years had debilitated the Jews, and they capitulated for lack of arms and men. One grim day, the Romans mounted the walls of Jerusalem with battering rams and portable bridges and charged into the streets of the city. They set fire to the Temple, then raped and massacred with a vengeance. Those Jews who were not slaughtered on the spot were taken to Rome and sold as slaves. The Legions staged a spectacular parade of triumph

in Rome, and special coins were struck in remembrance—
solemn honors reserved for victories over mighty enemies.
They built the great Triumphal Arch of Titus, which still
stands, and led Jerusalem's defenders through it in chains.

The fall of Jerusalem, in effect, marked the end of the
Jewish Commonwealth. The Romans were now free to turn
their attention to the few pockets of resistance that still held
out in the land. This required two more years of mopping-up,
and then a legion, under the command of Flavius Silva, was
sent to take the fortress of Masada. Everything else in Judea
had fallen. Masada was the Jew's last citadel.

　　　*　　　　　*　　　　　*

It is fascinating to speculate why Rome, the dread ruler of
the world, was so gravely concerned, so determined to quell
the Jews. It was, after all, a gallant but hopeless uprising by
a small people, in a corner of the vast Roman Empire. The
answer seems clear. The conquered nations that made up the
Empire watched unbelieving as the Jews, singlehanded, for
four years and more, took on the Roman Goliath. If the Jews
succeeded in ousting the Romans, there were excellent prospects that the subjected Empire would ignite in revolt. A
victory of the Jews would reveal that Imperium Romanum
was not invincible.

　　　*　　　　　*　　　　　*

Flavius Silva, the Roman commander, set up his camp and
the long agony of Masada began. He built his main site on
the western side of Masada and threw a wall around all of the
fortress to make escape impossible. For three years he tried
in vain to storm the stronghold. By then the besieging
Romans had swelled to ten thousand men. They lived in
eight camps in the valley, whose sites are still visible today.

Then the determined Flavius Silva began a remarkable
feat of military engineering. On the rocky ledge, four hun-

dred fifty feet below the level of the fortress, he had his soldiers pile earth until they had raised a solid base three hundred feet high. On this he erected a pier of fitted stones, reaching seventy-five feet higher still. On this, in turn, the Romans raised heavy siege guns and a ninety-foot ironclad tower, with light artillery at the top.

Every day, for months, the doomed men and women within Masada gazed down over their walls. They saw the Romans below laboriously erecting an ever-rising mound that inched closer and closer to the top of the fortress. The Jews delayed the Romans with volleys of stones, but they knew this could never save them.

One day, the Romans' tower stood higher than the walls of Masada itself. The legionnaires now hauled up a great battering ram. Its huge stone ball smashed up and back against Masada's walls until they began to buckle. The beleaguered Jews devised a clever way of defeating the ram's purpose. They built an inner wall of wooden beams, and filled in earth between the new inner wall and the outer wall which the Romans were pounding. Now, each blow of the ram only strengthened and compressed the earth between the two walls.

The Romans halted, and a furious Flavius Silva realized that he would need other means to take the Jews. He ordered his men to catapult burning torches within the fortress. Soon flames licked along the walls of Masada, and then the wind suddenly turned and blew the fire back toward the Romans. According to Josephus, the Jews held their breath, as it seemed that a new miracle of fire would save them. But the wind changed again, and flames destroyed one wall of Masada, which crashed with a roar, leaving the defenders exposed.

The exultant Romans returned to their camp, and made their plans to enter the proud fortress the next morning.

*   *   *

The commander of the Jewish camp was an extraordinary man named Eliazar Ben Yair. He knew that all was lost. The next day the Romans would pour in, and every Jewish man, woman, and child would be killed or taken prisoner. He gathered his men about him and calmly proposed that they preserve their freedom to the last. They would cheat the Romans of their victory by setting Masada aflame, and then dying by their own hand.

Josephus records that Ben Yair urged his men to take their own lives, as well as those of their wives and children, sooner than be slaughtered or taken into slavery by the Romans. Ben Yair reminded his hearers of what had happened to those Jews who had been captured by the enemy in other strongholds.

It must have been a gravely emotional scene. The trapped band of Zealots, Essenes, and Sicarii daggermen, wretched, filthy, and sick after three years of holding off the Romans, listened to Eliazar Ben Yair's chilling proposal. To die at the hand of an enemy is one thing; deliberately to kill one's loved ones, and then oneself, is another.

Josephus, in his famous book *The Jewish War,* reconstructs Eliazar's speech with deeply felt prose. It almost seems as though the eloquence of Josephus in these pages is an expiation for his own role as a turncoat. Josephus himself had been a leader of the Jewish Army in Galilee and had gone over to the Romans. Eliazar Ben Yair is clearly the man that the former Jewish general Josephus would have wanted to be. He cites Eliazar as saying, "Those who died in battle we may well congratulate; they died defending their freedom, not betraying it." On those who survived: "Old men with streaming eyes sit by the ashes of the Shrine of Jerusalem with a few women kept by the enemy as victims of their lust. Let us deny the enemy their hope for pleasure at our expense, and without any more ado leave them to be dumbfounded by our death and awed by our courage."

Eliazar Ben Yair must have been a leader of remarkable powers of persuasion. The desperate men within Masada listened tensely to their commander asking them to commit suicide. Then, with a strange exaltation, they prepared their families.

"For at the very moment when with streaming eyes they embraced and caressed their wives, and taking their children into their arms they pressed their last lingering kisses, hands other than their own seemed to assist them," Josephus records.

The terrible deed began. "They then chose ten men by lot out of them, to slay all the rest, every one of whom lay himself down by his wife and children on the ground, and threw his arms about them, and they offered their necks to the stroke of those who by lot executed that melancholy office; and when those ten had, without fear, slain them all, they made the same rule of casting lots for themselves, that he whose lot it was should kill the other nine, and after all, should kill himself."

It was nearly dawn. The Romans would soon arrive. "So finally the nine presented their throats, and the one man left till last first surveyed the serried ranks of the dead, in case amidst all the slaughter someone was still in need of his hand; then finding that all had been dispatched, set the place blazing fiercely and summoning all his strength drove his sword right through his body and fell dead by the side of his family."

Nine hundred and sixty men, women, and children lay dead. Only two old women and five children survived, who had somehow managed to hide themselves.

Early next morning the troops of Flavius Silva, coming in full armor to the attack, "were met with a terrible solitude on every side." Finding no sign of life, they shouted aloud. The two women crept forward and informed the stunned Romans "what had been done as it had been done." The defenders of Masada had even left the food in the storehouses intact, as a message to the Romans—the Jews had not done this thing because they were starving; they had done it to remain proudly free men. Skeptical at first, the Romans soon found the piled bodies.

In the late 1930's, in British-governed Palestine, a young student called Avraham Stern became the coinitiator of the Jewish underground terrorist band, called the "Irgun." Stern was later killed by the British. In the "Irgun" he had used the alias, Eliazar Ben Yair.

In July 1969, Israeli soldiers gave heroes' burials to some of the 960 defenders who perished in the historic suicide pact on Masada 1,896 years ago.

The remains of twenty-seven men, women, and children found on the rock fortress near the Red Sea by archeologists were interred with full military honors at Masada, near the ramp their Roman besiegers had built for the attack on the fortress.

Every year the Israeli Army holds solemn, torch-lit, swearing-in ceremonies on top of Masada. Groups of youngsters hike there every spring, in pilgrimage. In the 1940's, in the underground days, there was no easy tourist road to ascend, as there is today; you went up the treacherous side along the ancient "Snake Path," hanging onto a rope, and one fatal slip could mean plunging more than a thousand feet below. Over the years, several youngsters died while climbing Masada. Others were ambushed trying to get there along the lonely approaches: the hikers were easy victims for Arab and Bedouin snipers perched behind high rocks. The British still held Palestine then, and it was forbidden for Jews to carry weapons even for self-defense.

Yet year after year the sabras kept coming to Masada and climbing to its parapets, despite the danger. It was not an uncommon sight to see a young father carrying his small son on his back. One army officer returned in this fashion, spring after spring, until the boy was sturdy enough to make the mystical ascent on his own feet.

After Jerusalem herself, no place holds more emotional impact for young Israelis; and for many, Masada is *the* place.*

It must be remembered that there have really been no national heroes among the Jews since the Jews lost their nation. There have been no end of thinkers, such as Spinoza and Einstein, but no Cromwell, no Joan of Arc, no Washington to fire a young lad's imagination. That is why the sabra eagerly reaches across nineteen hundred years and loves the epic of Masada. "It is a savage tale, this story of the last Hebrew fortress, and yet strangely soothing." It has the grimly satisfying catharsis of high tragedy, and gives poetry to the sabra's own embattled life. And Masada and the Jewish War fulfill another profound need for the young Israeli, they are his reply to the shameful charge that Jews have always allowed themselves to be meekly slaughtered.

The sabra's fascination with Masada is clearly because of his need for roots. To paraphrase the quotation by Koestler at the opening of this chapter, the lost bride has been found, remarried, and is husbanded with the fierce attention for which Semetic husbands are famous.

There are other manifestations of this root-mystique: the obsession with Jerusalem, with archeology, and with the Bible. When ancient Jerusalem was unexpectedly captured

---

* This fascination with Masada seems to have bemused people abroad, as well, Jews and Gentile alike. In 1963, and again in 1964, the sabra archeologist-general Yigal Yadin launched a full-scale excavation at Masada, which until then had been almost untouched by the spade. Yadin was deluged with would-be volunteers, from all walks of life, from all over the world, begging to be allowed to join the dig, at their own expense.

during the Six Days' War, the sabras went mad. They became as maudlin about the return of the City of David as did the most sentimental old Jews.

In a famous radio broadcast during that war, when the sabra radio reporter went with the first troops into the Old City of Jerusalem, he cried with hysteria and exultation in his voice, "Ladies and gentlemen—I am not a religious person —I am not even what you call traditional—but our soldiers are at The Wall! The Wall is again in Jewish hands!"

He broke down and wept. And the whole country, gathered around their radios, wept with him, old tremblers, Marxists, and sabras alike. (And please don't call it the Wailing Wall; that smacks of Yiddish breast-beating; the sabras refer to it grandly and accurately, as the outer Wall of King Solomon's Temple.)

Similar public displays of sentiment by the usually tight-lipped sabras was to be heard in a dozen interviews after the Six Days' War.

"The Western Wall had been taken. On my transistor I heard the blasts of Rabbi Goren's ram's horn while soldiers at the Wall were crying. It made me feel as if I had suddenly returned to some place I had previously known but had forgotten about."

"It gradually dawned on me that we were going to capture the Old City. When I realized it, chills ran through me."

"We have resumed political control of Jerusalem in its entirety after nineteen centuries of dispossession. After nineteen years of exclusion by the Jordanians, we are back in the Old City."

"Until the sixth of June, the Wall to me was something obscurely associated with pictures in books or on copper plates—a stone wall, moss growing out of its chinks, with Jews praying and weeping beside it. . . . After we took the Wall, I just had to touch the stones. I saw some friends, paratroopers, standing beside me next to the Wall, praying and clasping the stones. It's a queer feeling, suddenly."

"Anyone standing there watching us converge on the Wall, anyone watching that steel-helmeted mass surging down, column after column, may have echoed in his head the same biblical passage that sang in my heart: 'They shall walk after the Lord, he shall roar like a lion.' "

All this emotionalism about Jerusalem is hardly surprising. After all, for two thousand years devout Jews throughout the world have prayed daily for the return of Jerusalem, and vowed, "If I forget thee, Oh Jerusalem."

The pragmatic sabra, by and large, shrugged at this before the Six Days' War. But you could not be an Israeli during that struggle against the biblical enemy, the Egyptians, without hearing the fluttering of angels' wings about you and the clanging of Jehovah's terrible swift sword. The brooding hills of Jerusalem took on a special mystic quality that caused tremors even among athiests. This air was supernatural, heaven was real; and if a white-bearded prophet brandishing his pikestaff appeared over the horizon, it would have seemed the most natural of events.

"In Israel, archeology is a seeking for confirmation of roots," Yigal Yadin, the noted sabra general and archeologist of Masada has written. "We are digging into the motherland, back to the womb."

Archeology is almost a national passion among the Israelis. It is discussed everywhere, with the knowledgeability of conversations about food in France, or opera in Italy. People from all walks of life dig, as pastime—farmers, taxi drivers, doctors, members of Knesset, and army generals. (It is free, which for the hard-pressed Israelis adds to its appeal.)

The Bible is the sabra's extended autobiography; it is his

link between a generation-old nation and a four-thousand-year-old culture.

But this usually has little to do with religion. Less than 30 per cent of Israelis are devout Jews. Rather, it is a love of the archetype in the Jungian sense: the inherited idea derived from the experiences of the race and present in the unconscious of the individual.

It may or may not be true that an obscure desert god called Jehovah liberated a certain stubborn tribe from Egypt, entered into covenant with them, and led them to the land of Canaan. But for even the non-religious sabra, the story is very important. This is because the Bible means far more to him than it means to other Jews. He loves it, and reads it constantly. In a manner quite incredible to foreigners, the Bible is for the sabras a contemporary volume of intense topical interest. It is also his history, his literature, and a book of excellent reference as to how to deal—consciously or unconsciously—with the pressing problems of today.

Unlike most Jews in other countries, the sabra likes to know who he is and where he came from. The Bible tells him. The young Israeli prides himself on the long history of Jewish kings, warriors, and prophets, with the same smug satisfaction that, say, the British rejoice in their glittering parade of Plantagenet and Tudor rulers. David and Solomon, Judas Maccabeus, Eliazar of Masada—these are real historic figures for the sabra, far more meaningful to him than the personae of the last two thousand years of Jewish history.

Gilboa is not only where his army unit bivouaced on maneuvers, it is where great King Saul, first King of Israel, anointed by the prophet Samuel, beloved of David, died in battle.

And the town of Ashkalon is not only near where David slew the giant Goliath, and near where Samson was betrayed to the Philistines by Delilah, it is the place where the sabra took his holiday last summer and the hotel was overpriced and the beds lumpy. Ashkalon is also not far from Masada.

For the sabra, Fortress Israel and Fortress Masada are clearly one. They are grimly linked across the centuries and face a common peril. When a young Israeli climbs to the top of Masada and walks about its parapets and stares at the still visible mound where Flavius Silva's legion built its assault tower, there is a sense of tragic unity between the new and the ancient defenders of Israel. Past and present, unfortunately, seem much the same.

Unless the casual visitor to Israel is very observant, he is not aware that all Israel is a fortress. People seem reasonably cheerful, they sit in cafés and pack the cinemas. The newspapers are calm. But in wartime, each town, each village, each settlement, becomes a little bristling fortress in itself. Trenches are manned, duties assigned, and foodstocks are distributed. Able-bodied men vanish within hours into the citizen-army, along with trucks, private cars, buses, and everything on wheels. Emergency arrangements at once begin to carry on essential services. In the suburb of Herzlia, where the present writers live, during the Six Days' War pools of women collected garbage, and solemn children delivered the mail on bicycles.

One day a team of zealous American sociologists ought to do research in Israel on the effects of a life of constant physical insecurity upon young people. Since the day the first Zionist settler came to Palestine and had children, the sabras have grown up in a day-to-day climate of tension, danger, and profound uncertainty. It has been a life of strange running battles that were fought rather quietly, and then erupted savagely into sudden open warfare with the Arabs. It is a life utterly different from the life of the rest of Western society today. It is no-peace, the life of Fortress Israel.

The Israeli child absorbs this sense of constant danger with his mother's milk, so to say. He does not talk about it much, because nobody else talks about it. But he knows that before the new borders provided by the Six Days' War, there were few villages in Israel where an Arab shell could not reach with ease. If the young sabra lives in a kibbutz along the border, his kindergarten moves into underground bunkers when the sirens go off, and his parents feel quieter when he sleeps there.

The Arabs are always there as a menacing backdrop, interrupting your life. You have to sacrifice your summer vacation because your army's unit is doing eight weeks' training this year instead of the usual four. It looks serious again; your husband will probably be called up if the "incidents" go on along the border. With a sigh you put off your plans for that dinner party. The children wanted to go camping on Lake Tiberias, but there's been shelling from the Syrians up there. . . .

The amazing thing is that all this is accepted quite matter-of-factly, with little emotion. Life simply goes on. The children in the kibbutzim become even attached to their underground shelters, and laugh and play there. But of course, the child is profoundly affected. Recently, in an Israeli class, a teacher asked her charges to write a composition on "My Most Unforgettable Day." Whereas in another land these reports would be concerned, perhaps, with a fishing trip, or a ride on a roller-coaster, young sabras wrote about "The day my father almost stepped on a mine," "The day the army took away all the buses."

This nonpeace way of life of modern Israel may not be altogether harmful. It has produced the tough, resilient young Israelis, who have the stamina that determines whether or not a nation lives or dies. Tension and danger can serve a useful role in the making of a new nation.

And after all, Jews have really endured a nonpeace for two thousand years, and are alive and kicking.

The sabra knows all this, but would much prefer the quiet life of, say, Switzerland, even though the playwright Durenmatt has pointed out that Switzerland's long centuries of peace have given the world two remarkable things: Gruyère cheese and the cuckoo clock. The sabra is proud that two thousand years of Jewish nonpeace have given the world a long list of geniuses, from Jesus to Marx and Freud. But he would welcome the chance to live, for a while at least, without geniuses, in a land of peace and cuckoo clocks.

*   *   *

During the grave fortnight before the Six Days' War, death and catastrophe were very much on peoples' minds in Israel. Arab unity, which had been called "a madman's notion," had occurred. With chilling awareness, Israelis watched Egypt, Syria, and Jordan become united for the first time in many years. Strategically, modern Israel had always lived with the nightmare of encirclement, and now the nightmare was reality.

There was little doubt, for the Israelis, that swift annihilation would follow, as had happened under the Romans and the Nazis, and as the Arabs promised now. Israelis calmly prepared to die, if necessary. Under no circumstances would they allow themselves to be taken again into captivity for later slaughter as Jews were taken in Europe during 1940–45.

In Tel Aviv, cinemas and public halls were set up as emergency hospitals for the expected minimum ten thousand casualties of the Arab attack. (By size of population, ten thousand Israeli dead is comparable to one million American dead.) In Herzlia, the two young sabra children of the present writers helped dig slit trenches in the back yard of our home.

This was not mere alarmism. Anyone living in Israel has

only to open his radio to Cairo, Damascus, and Jordan and listen to the lurid blood lust that pours out daily, crying for total destruction of Israel. On June 1, 1967, Ahmed Shukairy, the chieftain of the Palestine Liberation Organization (who later fled in battle when war began), gave an interview in the Jordanian section of Jerusalem. Asked what would happen to sabras, native-born Israelis, if the Arab attack succeeded, he replied: "Those who survive will remain in Palestine. But, estimate that none of them will survive."

There were many similar Arab declarations, and the Israelis knew exactly what defeat would mean.* As Eliazar Livneh, one of our keenest observers, wrote after the Six Days' War:

For the Jews of the Diaspora (abroad) to say nothing of Western man as a whole, the Jewish Holocaust at the hands of the Germans is a thing of the past, a closed chapter. The Jews of Israel, however, have been made to realize that the Holocaust is an ever present danger. For them, the struggle of the 60's against the Arabs is simply a continuation of the struggle of the 40's against the Germans, under a different guise.

In the Six Days' War, the Israelis smashed the Arabs with incredible speed, so that an impression arose in the world that it was mere child's play for the Israelis. It was nothing of the kind. One of the largest tank battles of all time (comparable to those which took place on the Russian front during World War II) occurred in the Sinai Peninsula, with Egypt throwing a thousand tanks against the Israelis. It was also the epic of a citizen-army closing ranks against the com-

---

* The best-selling record in Israel after the Six Days' War was nothing less than collected tapes of speeches from Radio Cairo beamed toward Israel in the weeks before the war (in fractured Hebrew): "Jews! We are coming to drive you all into the sea. Prepare to die! We are going to butcher you and no one can save you this time; Moshe Dayan will lose his other eye!" etc.

mon peril to a remarkable degree. There was astounding heroism displayed at the front, and a heady spirit of self-sacrifice at home, as Fortress Israel was again endangered. These were the deeds that saved Israel, but there were other reasons. There was the knowledge that this was truly a war of survival, as every Jewish war against the Arabs always is. If Israel were to defeat the Arab states fifty times, they would not cease to exist; but it is quite enough for the Arabs to defeat Israel only once and there will be no Israel. There was the grim determination summed up in the rallying cry "Never Again." Every Jew has been in Auschwitz; the Israeli Jews above all were haunted by the traumatic memory.

There was the desperate fear that this new, precious Jewish state would prove to be (as Ben-Gurion has often brooded) but another gallant episode in the Jews' four-thousand-year-old history. A wild but hopeless burst of freedom before the Jews were driven homeless once again. Another Jewish-Roman War, another Masada. The lost bride, the Israelis vowed, would not be snatched away again.

CHAPTER III

Hebrew, Speak Hebrew!
The Children of Ben Yehuda

✡ "A language is a dialect that has an army and a navy."
—Max Weinrich

The most remarkable thing about the sabra—except for the still incredible fact that he is a citizen of a Jewish state—is that he speaks Hebrew. This is fantastic. It is a major miracle in a land not unaccustomed to miracles, and which has always been on familiar terms with the supernatural. What makes it extraordinary that Israeli children speak Hebrew as naturally as French children speak French, as casually as Greek speak Greek, is the stupendous fact that Hebrew had been a dead language for two thousand years.

In 1882, in Jerusalem, for the first time in more than twenty centuries, an infant came into the world hearing no language but Hebrew. This famous cultural test-tube sabra thereupon spoke the ancient biblical tongue from the cradle up. The Jews of Palestine were flabbergasted by this achievement.

The child's father was an utterly possessed fanatic named Eliazer Perlman. He was a frail, penniless, gravely tubercular schoolteacher from Lithuania. At the age of twenty-two, Perlman had been forced to abandon his medical studies at the Sorbonne because of poor health. He converted to Zionism a full generation before Theodor Herzl burst like a comet on the scene. Among the forces that influenced Perlman was the English novelist George Sand's flaming novel *Daniel Deronda,* a Jewish-nationalistic tract by a Gentile which excited many Jews to the Zionist cause. Perlman decided to go and live in the Land.

This was a startling decision for an enlightened young Jew in the 1880's, but Perlman was a revolutionist. (He once remarked that his first political act was to speak Hebrew in a Paris bistro.) The quixotic, impossible cause he championed was nothing less than reviving Hebrew and persuading all Jews to speak it in their everyday lives. The fact that Hebrew had only some eight thousand words, and was as equipped for the modern world as the English of Beowulf would be today, did not bother him in the least. The words that were missing, the tens of thousands of meanings that a living tongue would have naturally developed over two millenia, Perlman calmly decided to invent. He was not a philologist, not even a linguist. He was merely a mad Zionist, intoxicated with private vision of a race of sabras: Hebrew-speaking Hebrews.

He launched his attack at home. He refused to address, or to be addressed by, a Jew in any language but Hebrew. He gave himself a Hebrew name, Ben Yehuda, which means "son of Judea." He commanded his Russian-born wife to converse only in Hebrew with him, although she knew not a syllable. He taught her. They became the only two people, at least in the entire Western world, who spoke Hebrew as their daily language.

When his wife was pregnant, Ben Yehuda made her take a solemn vow not to let their baby hear any "contaminating foreign dialects." The child of Ben Yehuda was to be, in effect, a pilot sabra. A boy was born and placed in its mother's arms. *"Yaldi!"* (My child!) cried its mother. Thus, as every thoroughly bored youngster in Israel learns today, Deborah Yonas Ben Yehuda, the daughter of a wine distiller from Glubokia, became the first mother in two thousand years to address her child in the resurrected language of the Israelites.

The great experiment began. Ben Yehuda, with fanatical zeal, thought of everything. He stood at the nursery door and carefully screened all friends and relatives who wished to enter. Only those who were able to speak Hebrew (which most Jews knew as the sacred tongue for liturgical services) and who were willing to do so in the child's presence were allowed to enter. Servants who had to come into the room, but who were ignorant of Hebrew and spoke instead Yiddish or whatever, went about their tasks in silence under Ben Yehuda's forbidding eye.

A year went by and the child did not speak. Ben Yehuda was jeered and savagely attacked by the Jewish community of Jerusalem, who were up in arms against him for profaning the Holy Tongue. Pious Jews revered Hebrew as a kind of esoteric Esperanto to be spoken only while appealing to the Deity. They were content to leave Hebrew hibernating in its historical deepfreeze and dismissed Ben Yehuda's schemes as the warped dream of a lunatic. Ben Yehuda fought them off and spent all his free time compiling Hebrew words and inventing new words that a child of the modern world would need. Much more than one child's speech was at stake. Ben Yehuda believed that the fight for Hebrew was the fight for Zionism. Hebrew was the tool par excellence to weld a people arriving from a hundred lands. His motives were down to earth as well as mystic: there had to be one common language, one common denominator for all who would come.

A second long year went by, and the child still did not

speak, yet still heard only Hebrew. The situation grew tense. Friends of Ben Yehuda, even those who were ardent Hebraists themselves, urged him to abandon his experiment. He was solemnly warned that he was turning his child into an idiot. A man of iron will, despite his slight body with its malignant disease, Ben Yehuda refused to yield. It seemed to him that his experiment was fraught with destiny, that the entire future of the Jewish people was at stake.

"If we want our children to be Hebrews," he wrote passionately in his struggling Hebrew newspaper, *The Deer*, "we must train them in the Hebrew language. We must make our sons and daughters forget the corrupt foreign dialects that tear us to shreds and undermine our unity as a people, thus rendering us an object of scorn among the nations."

The child had its third birthday and still produced no intelligible sound. The opposition to Ben Yehuda grew really fierce now. The devoutly religious, devoutly anti-Zionist Jewish community of Jerusalem was as rabid and tough as was Ben Yehuda himself. They spoke Yiddish among themselves, or Ladino, or whatever language or argot had been spoken in the Gentile country from which they had come. It was perfectly clear to them that the Deity strongly disapproved of Ben Yehuda and was punishing his child. A spewing infant that was encouraged to prattle in the Holy Tongue of sages and scholars! The lofty language in which revered rabbis pondered the mysteries of good and evil, the soul, eternity, and other sublime matters! The awesome speech in which Jehovah Himself had addressed Abraham and Moses! What had this to do with diapers and vegetables and children's games?

At last, well into his third year, the son of Ben Yehuda spoke. They were probably the most eagerly awaited words from an infant's lips since King Psammetichus had ordered a child isolated in a cave from birth, in order to learn from its first remarks which was the most primeval of tongues. The sabra Ben Zion (son of Zion) Ben Yehuda spoke not in French, nor in English, nor in German, nor in Russian, nor in Polish, nor in Arabic, nor in Yiddish, which is a crude medieval German, nor in Ladino, which is the Judeo-Spanish dialect spoken by the descendants of the Jews who were expelled from Spain after the Inquisition, nor in the Judeo-Arabic dialect of the Jews of North Africa and Yemen, nor in the Judeo-Persian dialect of the Jews from Persia, Afghanistan, and Bokhara, nor in neo-Aramaic, which is a modern version of the language of Jesus, as well as of the diplomats of the ancient Middle East, and which is still spoken by the Jews of Syria and Kurdistan, nor in the Aramaic-Arabic mixture spoken by the Jews of Libya, nor in the dozen of splinter-languages spoken by such exotic Jewish communities as the Falashas of Ethiopia, the ancient Krimchak Jews of the Crimea, and the Cochin Jews of India, who probably arrived on the Malabar coast around 70 A.D., fleeing from Roman persecution after the fall of Jerusalem.

The man-child of Ben Yehuda spoke Hebrew as naturally as a Frenchman speaks French. His father had proved that it could be done. Through his "holy stubborness," Hebrew was to flourish in one of the most spectacularly successful cultural revolutions in history. As one ecstatic admirer put it, "Hebrew stirred and awoke full-throated, out of the caverns of memory and the mute written word." The great revival was on.

*   *   *

Palestine in 1880, the year Ben Yehuda arrived, was an unappetizing place. Palestine was an ignored, corner of the ramshackle and sickly Turkish Ottoman Empire. The governing pashas were corrupt and cruel. There was already a scattered handful of isolated Jewish agricultural settlements, but most Jews lived in the orthodox quarters of the four Jewish Holy cities of medieval Palestine: Jerusalem, Safed, Tiberias, and Hebron. Three quarters of the Palestinian Jews were Sepharadim (from Spain and Oriental lands) and they spoke mainly the dialect Ladino, and Arabic. The rest of the Jewish community were "Ashkenazim," of chiefly eastern European background, and they spoke Yiddish, the dialect of the ghettos of Poland and Russia.

Jerusalem herself was a mosaic of perpetually quarreling religious and ethnic groups, living in separate quarters, bound together by sanctity and a lively mutual hatred. In the Old City, the core of Jerusalem, there was a Moslem, an Armenian, a Christian, and a Jewish quarter. Soleiman's Wall surrounded the Old City, and beyond the gates of old Jerusalem was the new Jewish quarter called *Mea Shearim,* The Hundred Gates. This quarter had been built in the 1870's, and here came ancient and pious Jews from all over the world, not to live, but to die. They handed over their lifetime savings to the *Kehillah,* the Jewish community, in exchange for a yearly pittance until the day of their death. They had not come to be reborn, as did the Zionists, but rather because the devout held it to be a blessing to die in the Holy Land. When the Messiah came, riding on his white mule, those Jews who had gasped their last breath in Palestine would be first resurrected.

The Jews of Jerusalem survived on philanthropic alms sent by pious Jews from abroad and supplemented their half-starving existence by making olive-wood trinkets of the Holy Land. They prayed and pondered the Book, and quarreled passionately among themselves, and tried to use *Kaballah,* the ancient metaphysical lore, to induce the Messiah to come quickly and alleviate the misery of the Jews.

The years passed, and the Messiah still did not come. A sturdy new generation had grown up in Mea Shearim—fierce-eyed men who stalked purposefully in black kaftans and fur hats, and round women with shorn heads and wigs. The elders of Jerusalem begot children at fine patriarchal ages, and the new generation, no less godly and prolific, usually produced a brood of eight or twelve offspring. Whole families lived and slept in one room, and shared kitchens and toilets and balconies with their neighbors, and dwelt in blessed squalor.

Life revolved gravely about the Sabbath, and the Jewish holidays, which celebrated the Jewish past, and about the near future, when the Messiah would come. He was expected, momentarily, from month to month. These Jews ate bitter herbs in remembrance of the Exodus from Egypt, they fasted on the desolate day of the Temple's destruction, they blew the ram's horn wildly on Yom Kippur, the Day of Atonement, to open the gates of heaven, and they got drunk once a year in joyful recollection of the biblical Queen Esther's triumph over the despot Haman.

In Jerusalem, women were not permitted to speak Hebrew. Some of the enlightened planters of Palestine taught their girls French, but God forbid, not Hebrew, nor Jewish History and literature. Such contamination, it was correctly feared, would make the impressionable girls susceptible to that mad scheme, the Zionist idea.

Zionism was thoroughly unpopular among the old-timers. They abhorred the new pioneers like Ben Yehuda, who had begun to arrive in the country in tiny numbers, as atheistic nationalists who blasphemed against God's Eternal Will. The patriarchs found it absurd for a Jew to determine his own destiny. The Messiah, the Deliverer, would do that.

This was the life of most Jews in Palestine when the young Zionist fanatic Eliazer Ben Yehuda arrived with his worldly young bride.

*   *   *

Ben Yehuda, a born fighter if there ever was one, was soon battling with every authority in sight. He helped launch a school for girls, in which subjects would be taught in Hebrew, and he was attacked in the streets for defiling the Tongue of Angels and Prophets. He was reviled as Ben Alamek, the son of Alamek, the traditional archenemy of the Jews. He went on, never missing a chance to preach his gospel. Once when Ben Yehuda was conversing with his wife in the street, he was stopped by a stranger.

"Excuse me, sir," the stranger asked in Yiddish, "that language you are speaking, What may it be?"

"Hebrew."

"But people do not speak Hebrew; it's a dead language!"

"You are wrong, my friend," Ben Yehuda replied with fervor. "I am alive. My wife is alive. We speak Hebrew, therefore Hebrew is alive."

Coughing his lungs out, living in abject poverty, Ben Yehuda was denounced to the Turks as a firebrand and spent a week in jail. When his second son was born, he could not afford a bottle of wine for the occasion. He went on with his monumental thesaurus of Hebrew, and also created thousands upon thousands of new words. Slowly, the cause of Hebrew made progress, and in 1888 came the first major breakthrough: Hebrew was adopted as the language for teaching of all subjects at the elementary school of one staunchly Zionist village. Other schools gradually succumbed to Hebrew, although the religious authorities put both pupils and parents on a blacklist.

Ben Yehuda helped organize the "Army of the Defenders of the Language," which met secretly in a Jerusalem attic, and whose credo read: "The members will watch in the streets and when they hear Jews speaking Russian, French, Arabic, and so on, they will not spare a remark even to the eldest of them, and will cry out, 'Are you not ashamed?' "

It took some seventy years, but by the birth of Israel in 1948 it had become indeed almost shameful for a Jew to speak a foreign language in a public place in Israel.

Eventually his enemies censored Ben Yehuda for one of his spirited attacks on what he called "the parasitical Jews" of Jerusalem, who lived on alms from abroad, instead of becoming pioneers on the land. This was too much. An awesome *herem*, or ban of excommunication, was imposed on Ben Yehuda, complete with ancient rites that included the burning of black candles in the synagogues. A town crier walked slowly through the chalk-dusty streets of Jerusalem, blowing a ram's horn and denouncing Ben Yehuda. It was now forbidden for any good Jew to read or possess Ben Yehuda's Hebrew newspaper.

Although stricken with tuberculosis at an early age, Ben Yehuda lived, through sheer determination, until he was sixty-five. But his devoted wife soon caught the disease from him and died. The religious authorities saw a new revenge: Ben Yehuda was a heretic, and therefore the body of his wife was unclean. They refused to bury her in a Jewish cemetery and relented only after an uproar by partisans of her husband.

By the time of his death in 1914, Ben Yehuda had completed five fat volumes of his monumental dictionary. By 1918 there were 85,000 Jews in Palestine, and 40 per cent of them spoke Hebrew in their daily lives. Almost singlehandedly, Ben Yehuda had rescued Hebrew from its holy petrifaction and created the modern Hebrew language.

*   *   *

"How shall we speak to each other?" Herzl wrote in his utopian and prophetic book, *The Jewish State*. "We certainly will not talk Hebrew."

Theodor Herzl was a brilliant Hungarian journalist who

discovered the depths of his own Jewishness while covering the Dreyfus case in Paris for his newspaper in Vienna. He burst upon the Zionist world like a whirlwind with his startling books, which proposed nothing less than a Jewish nation reborn. This idea electrified Jews who had until then been indifferent to the Zionist idea, and dazzled those like Ben Yehuda who had already gone to live in Palestine. Herzl's little time bomb called *The Jewish State* proved to be one of the seminal books which alter the course of history. Its appearance in 1896 launched Zionism on a meaningful scale.

One of the fascinating things about Zionism is the small army of hot-eyed fanatics who have served it. They were mystic, colorful, charismatic personalities who would have made their mark anywhere. To name but a few at random: A. D. Gordon, the ascetic who preached the religion of Jewish labor and in middle age went to Palestine to work with his hands and became the spiritual father of the kibbutz movement; Captain Orde Wingate,* the devout Christian soldier of the British Army who in the late 1930's trained the Jewish Night Squads that later became the nucleus of Haganah; Ben-Gurion, who has the driving spirit and single-mindedness and haloed hair of an Old Testament prophet; and Eliazer Ben Yehuda and Theodore Herzl.

Ben Yehuda decided to leave Jerusalem and seek out Herzl to induce this new powerful Zionist champion to endorse the crusade for Hebrew-speaking Hebrews. The meeting was almost impossible to arrange. Herzl had the ear of pashas, potentates, and Rothschilds, and poor Ben Yehuda had a difficult time just catching up with the journalist, who traveled incessantly, almost compulsively. (Herzl died in 1904, burned out and exhausted, at the age of forty-four.)

They met in Vienna, the two bearded, feverish prophets,

---

* In the 1948 war of Independence, Wingate's English widow circled above the Jewish soldiers in a small plane, and dropped Wingate's Bible to them.

but the meeting was a failure. Herzl was locked in his private dream: he was after the grand design of a Jewish state, and was quite indifferent to Hebrew. In fact, the notion made him uneasy. As with most *Mittel-europa* Jews, Herzl was most at home in German: at the first Zionist Congress that Herzl called, in 1897, most of the delegates spoke German as a matter of course. It was the cultured, honorable language of Goethe and Schiller. A secretary kept minutes of the florid orations of the Congress, and when an adamant Palestinian delegate got up and proceeded to speak in Hebrew, no one could follow. The minutes noted stiffly: "The speaker spoke in Hebrew."

The dapper, sophisticated, Western Jew Herzl listened to the slight schoolteacher Ben Yehuda, from the ghetto of Lithuania and the parochial city of Jerusalem, and thought Ben Yehuda daft, much as Herzl himself must have appeared to the august rulers he himself petitioned. The idea that Jews, those born linguists, those wanderers who spoke with ease three or four languages, should go through the trouble of resurrecting the one language they did *not* speak, struck him as folly.

"Which of us knows enough Hebrew to order a railway ticket?" Herzl once asked gloomily. Keenly disappointed, Ben Yehuda returned to Jerusalem; Herzl went on with his audiences with the German Kaiser and British and Russian ministers of state.

Both men won out with their dreams. And yet, the Zionist idea would have irresistibly swelled without Herzl, and Hebrew would have been certainly adapted in a Zionist Palestine without Ben Yehuda. Both men were the instruments of history. Both had tapped deep roots.

The Zionist pioneers' search for roots led inexorably to Hebrew: it is the original language of the Old Testament.

This appeal was profound and irresistible for these new Jews who wanted to become Hebrews.*

The youngsters who now sought out Palestine resolutely embraced Hebrew, corrected each other's mistakes, and spoke Hebrew with their comrades—a process that still goes on today among newcomers in Israel. They wanted to rid themselves of their distasteful, often tragic, European past, of which Yiddish was a constant reminder; "I became a Hebrew in order no longer to be a Yid," is a valid comment one still hears.

History lent a hand to Ben Yehuda's battle with the Balfour Declaration and the Allied victory in World War I; these spurred further waves of immigrants toward Palestine. One common language now became an urgent necessity, and the choice of Hebrew was both "logical mysticism and mystical logic." Palestine was handed by the League of Nations to Britain's benevolent care, and in 1921 the British Mandatory Government helped enormously by declaring Hebrew an

* The biblical appeal of Hebrew has often excited Gentiles as well; in *The American Language*, H. L. Mencken notes that after the American Revolution, some members of Congress wanted to throw out English and make the language of the Tribes of Israel the official language of the United States. The mind boggles at the road America might have taken if it had become a Hebrew-speaking nation of New-World sabras. Hebrew was revered by many of the early God-fearing American settlers, and later among American scholars. Cotton Mather's writings included a dissertation of Hebrew pronunciation. The first book printed in the colonies was the *Bay Psalm Book*, which was a rendering of the Hebrew Psalms. In 1777, Yale obliged all the freshmen to study Hebrew. Samuel Johnson, the first president of King's College, which grew into Columbia University, declared in 1759 that "Hebrew was a gentleman's accomplishment," and "as soon as a lad has learned to speak English well, it is much the best to begin a learned education with Hebrew, the mother of languages." At Harvard, a Hebrew oration was delivered annually at commencement until 1817.

William Bradford, second governor of Plymouth Colony, declared that he studied Hebrew most of all languages because he "would see with his own eyes the ancient Oracles of God in their native beauty." For the Puritans, Hebrew was the key to Bible study, and the Bible itself a rule of life and the revealed Will of God. America was Canaan, the Atlantic Ocean the Red Sea, and they themselves the persecuted Children of Israel.

official language of Palestine, together with English and Arabic, to be used as a matter of course in courts and government offices.

After World War II, refugees from the Nazi regime streamed into Palestine in unheard-of hundreds of thousands, and cities like Tel Aviv became an ever-mounting Tower of Babel with Yiddish, Roumanian, Polish, German, and just about every tongue known to man. By the year of the birth of the Jewish state in 1948, the Jewish community of Palestine had risen from 85,000 to 650,000. A census taken in that year revealed that 80 per cent of the Jews of Palestine could speak some Hebrew, and 54 per cent spoke *only* Hebrew in their daily lives.

Also in 1948, sixty-eight years after Eliazer Ben Yehuda arrived in Jerusalem, a full 92 per cent of the native-born Israelis—the sabras—spoke Hebrew as their mother tongue.

*   *   *

The sabras of Israel are children of Ben Yehuda as much as they are children of Herzl. They are the visible evidence of the victory of those men. And it was in the classrooms of Palestine that the battle for Hebrew was essentially won; every toddler who learned Hebrew at school became a potent propagandist Hebrew at home. The youngsters rebuked their greenhorn parents for speaking other languages; in public, the sabras were humiliated when addressed by their parents in a foreign mother-tongue. Even today, it is not uncommon for new settlers to address their youngster in Polish or English, or whatever, and for the sabra to reply curtly in Hebrew.

For the sabra, Israel is clearly divided into those who speak Hebrew naturally and those who do not. He cannot help feeling superior to those who speak it haltingly. He has been told since kindergarten age that true Hebrews speak Hebrew.

It is very much "in" to speak the rapid-fire Hebrew of the sabras; it is very much *declassé* not to. The sabra really does not speak Hebrew pleasingly; he speaks it harshly and gutterally. Many Hebrew philologists from abroad have complained, "But they are ruining the language!" Yet this very in-Hebrew of the sabra, with its layers of breezy slang and connotations, is the sabra's proud badge. It points up his sabra WASP-ness among the natives, and he feels paternalistic and rather colonial about "the others."

The sabra is inclined to be arrogant about Hebrew. Upon getting to know some new arrival, socially, he will ask, usually at the second meeting, "When are you going to do something about your Hebrew?" The sabra is not being intentionally rude; he feels sorry for these lesser Jews with lost identities, these poor devils wtih their hundred tongues of exile, who cling to their wretched jargons and argots. It all confirms his sense of being different. Jews speak anything; Hebrews speak Hebrew. This as much as anything else has widened the "we—Israeli," and "They—Jews" barrier.*

It is intriguing to muse what the modern sabra would be like if Hebrew had not been adopted. To conceive of the young Israeli speaking, say, Yiddish or English, or a free-for-all of languages, is impossible; altogether another individual emerges in the mind's eye, rather than the "New Hebrew" we know.

Hebrew, one of the world's oldest tongues, the tongue that God is said to have conferred on man when He created him, has clung stubbornly and defiantly to an alphabet that no stranger can read. The neophyte studying French or German has some frame of reference from his native English or Span-

---

* Abba Eban, who is Cambridge educated and vastly admired abroad, is not popular among most young Israelis. One reason for this is unquestionably Eban's overcultured, elegant, and entirely "un-sabra-like" Hebrew. It makes the sabras uncomfortable. Eban induces their awe, but not their confidence.

ish. He at least shares the same alphabet. But you cannot remotely guess at a page of Hebrew unless you study its alphabet. It is a closed world of its own.

Besides the problem of limited expression, and the foreign alphabet, the nonsabra approaching Hebrew soon learns to his horror that it is a language that consists only of consonants. Vowels are excluded. A system of vowel writing under the bewildering row of consonants was devised in the sixth and seventh centuries, but this is rarely used in print. Thus, you can determine neither the pronunciation nor the meaning of a given word until you have divined the approximate meaning of an entire phrase.* For example, the three printed letters DVD in the Hebrew alphabet can mean, according to the context used, either boiler, David, or the beloved one.

The sabra views these bewildering obstacles of his speech with perverse satisfaction. It is hard—so is working on a kibbutz under the searing sun, and so is fighting off eighty million Arabs. It is a soul-purifying challenge, along with everything else in Israel. The sabras, one sometimes feels, *like* being closed off, apart.

Hebrew was the speech of a hard-living, God-obsessed people, the Israelites. It is "a tongue of archaic ferocity; of wrath and thunderbolts and prophecies of damnation." You can make love or learn to play the flute in Hebrew, but not gracefully. Like Hungarian, it does not translate well into other languages, which may explain why the English-speaking world knows almost nothing of Israeli writing. Its abrupt limitations make translations into Hebrew embarrassingly

---

* The use of the complicated dot system under the consonants was already found to be cumbersome in the ninth century. Scholars approached the sage known as Natronai II, the Genius of Sura, and proposed that something be done about the mess. He replied firmly that the Tablets of the Law given to Moses on Sinai were without vowel signs, and what was good enough for the Deity was good enough for sinful man.

similar, and, say, Dickens and Kafka in Hebrew sound weirdly alike. Most American writers translate into an excellent parody of the terse, clipped style of Hemingway.

Often the sabra seems raw, unformed, and phlegmatic, and it has been suggested that the inchoate nature of Hebrew may contribute toward shaping these traits. It is as though all young Englishmen today by some quirk suddenly began speaking in the archaic rhythms and sparse vocabulary of Chaucer. They too would seem unleavened, abrupt, and deficient. Hebrew's last classic was the Old Testament. It has basically seen nothing, heard nothing, known nothing since Masada fell. Tens of thousands of new words have been invented by Ben Yehuda and his successors, but it all needs time to jell.

The sabra will shrug and answer you that Ben Yehuda found 8,000 words, and we now have over 40,000 and it's only a question of catching up. As with many other staggering problems of his land, he answers cockily, *Yehiyeh beseder—* "It will end up OK." In the meantime, with Jewish involuted pride and stubborness, he resists every effort to latinize his language and make Hebrew part of the world's cultural establishment. All efforts in this direction were doomed; a son of Ben Yehuda actually ran a Latin-alphabet Hebrew paper for a while, but its chances were nil. To latinize Hebrew would destroy its mystique. For those unfortunates who are not sabras, and who come to Israel in middle age, often more dead than alive, a life in an alien, Hebrew culture can be very hard. This is a language in which even after some years the foreigner reads a newspaper with difficulty, let alone literature.

This in turn has sharpened the cleavage between sabra and nonsabra; thousands of German and Mittel-europa Jewish intellectuals who arrived in Palestine in the 1930's, broken in spirit, gave up horrendous Hebrew after a few half-hearted tries and were doomed to an intellectual sterility for the rest of their days. You see them even now in Israel, with their ties and jackets in the sweltering heat, escaping from the frightening roar of Hebrew, sitting about with vacant eyes in émigré cafés where months-old journals from Frankfurt or Prague can be read for the price of an expresso. Refugees who arrive from the North African countries are also often sadly out of the swim; they have their own cafés where old American reruns on television from Lebanon are the entertainment, and where the café patrons relax in Arabic, and *nargilehs* pass with the coffee.

Unbearable loneliness can beset even the young, eager newcomer, caught in a swirl of a new land. What seemed idealistic back in London or Johannesburg can be vitiating and distressing in the reality of the hot streets of Tel Aviv. The urge is to run, get away to where one hears a reassuring tongue that one knows. The sabras themselves, passing by in careening, open truckloads, or sauntering down Dizengoff Road, can seem like gibbering Chinese.

And yet, of course, the majority of newcomers do master Hebrew, and are absorbed into the culture. Youngsters arriving usually are particularly anxious to become accepted as sabras and anxiously learn Hebrew. The government sponsors a ceaseless "Operation Hebrew," with nominal-cost, crash courses called "ulpan-Method," run by teachers who preach the gospel of Hebrew with the fever of missionaries. It is moving to watch ex-magistrates from Bucharest, ex-professors of law from Vienna, men with lifetimes of professional experience behind them, sweating out simple Hebrew phrases, exploding with joy when they get high marks, and taking part in simple classroom-Hebrew plays with the solemnity of youngsters. The Israeli Army is an all-persuasive teacher of Hebrew to new recruits, and even lends a hand by sending soldier-teachers to outlying villages to instill some Hebrew in immigrants who cannot write their name in any tongue.

* * *

Today learned graybeards sit in the Academy of the Hebrew Language and officially coin new words. Sometimes they take, and sometimes they don't. The scholars often mull over a new word for years before pronouncing it as final. Sometimes they "leak" the word to the press, to test public reaction. The Israelis roll the new word in their mouths, as Frenchmen do a new year of wine, and spit out their approval or denunciation.

But an equally important source of new words comes from the people themselves. It is almost a do-it-yourself parlor game, and any number can play. You follow the rules of construction from a three-letter biblical or semitic root, and you are on your own. Poets (who are deeply respected in Israel) coin new words monthly: it is considered to be one of their duties. The veteran poet Avraham Shlonsky alone has successfully introduced many new words into the stream of language. An enterprising journalist will invent a new word in an article and append a lengthy footnote explaining his sources. Many words enter in an underground way. A popular humorist and playwright, Efraim Kishon, was attacked not long ago by Dr. Gamzu, a weighty critic. Kishon struck back by coining the verb *gamaz,* to demolish, to lay out. The delighted Israeli public picked up the word at once.

The philologists, official and unofficial, breed new words and terms with the loving care of rose fanciers; The Israelis cock an eye and make up their minds whether or not to accept it. The Academy tried seven times with a word for "match," until *gafrur,* from *gafrit,* sulphur, caught hold. They gazetted a word "guard-children"; Israelis ignore it and prefer the Americanism, "baby-sitter."

Until lately there was no equivalent for that highly important twentieth-century term, frustration; the Academy neatly supplied *tiskul,* from the biblical root *sachol,* to thwart. Sometimes a foreign word is too strong in itself to submit to translation; the scholars in the beginning of the century wanted "speak far," but the Israelis ignore it and say *telefon.* To ring up someone is *letalphen.*

Sometimes the efforts of the Academy are downright brilliant. Ohm, Faraday, and Galvani were unknown to the Ten Tribes of Israel, but the prophet Ezekiel referred to a dazzling substance which he called *chashmal.* This became the Hebrew word for electricity, and through adroit juggling of prefixes and syntax there emerged *lechashmel,* to electrify, *chashmelan,* electrician, *chismul,* electrification, and *mechushmal,* electrocuted.

Sometimes the Bible is startlingly deficient in even humble words; for example, no cows seem to have been milked in ancient days. The only biblical reference is to the product itself, *chalav,* milk. Modern Hebrew blithely filled in a host of adjunctive terms, *lachalov,* to milk, *chaliva,* milking, *chalban,* milkman, and *machlava,* dairy.

The problems of inventing new terms, in a hurry, for physics, biology, automobiles, hydraulics, engineering, chemistry, business, politics, aeronautics, medicine, psychiatry, manufacturing, forestry, and all the other thousands of pursuits unknown to Abraham, Isaac, and Jacob defy the imagination. Here, the Academy has been rather successful, and whole dictionaries of terms for specific disciplines have been issued.

There are few curse words in Hebrew. This will come as a surprise to Bible lovers and ex-Sunday-school students who recall many vivid and bloodcurdling curses, couched in rolling and wrathful phrases. But by curse words we are referring to the short four-letter epithets by which the Anglo-

Saxon relieves his outraged soul and temper. For this need, the Israel of the 1920's and 1930's turned to Russian, and Slavic epithets relating to the addressee's mother were highly popular. Since the 1940's, and the coming of age of the sabras, Arabic has been the main source of earthy curses. This is explained by the close similarity in many basic words between the two Semitic languages. Mother is *ima* in Hebrew and *emma* in Arabic; father is *aba* in Hebrew, *abu* in Arabic; dog is *kelev* in Hebrew and *kalb* in Arabic. These three, adorned with adjectives, provide a serviceable fund of vivid invective.

Translators of Henry Miller, Norman Mailer, and other luminaries of American literature are therefore faced with grave handicaps. A popular humorist, the sabra Dan Ben Amoz, tried to fill the gap with a Hebrew dictionary of "dirty words," but it did not catch on.

Imagine the dilemma, therefore, when the Habimah Theatre in Tel Aviv, more noted for its Chekhov, decided to mount Albee's "Who's afraid of Virginia Woolf?" Besides the usual headaches of transcribing slang and in-phrases of another language, there were other problems. Hebrew contains hardly any of the rich, colorful synonyms for the male and female genitalia that most languages possess. It is very much a puritanical tongue, rather mid-Victorian in this respect. There is not even today an official word for mistress, unless you use the biblical term *pilegesh,* which means concubine. But this is unsatisfactory; a concubine is not a mistress. The "Virginia Woolf" translators were absolutely stumped for a Hebrew equivalent for "hump the hostess." After much feverish search they camp up with *l'dfok et hamarachat.* This means "to knock the hostess," and sounded fine. *L'dfok* itself is a quite innocent word, to knock; it is used daily in modern Israeli conversation with the connotation "to fix, to revenge" in an earthy way. Its onomatopoeic closeness to the famous

Anglo-Saxon four-letter word, which is universally known and employed, undoubtedly contributed to *l'dfok's* lusty adoption into Hebrew.

Thus, Hebrew grows and bounces along, borrowing new words with aplomb, inventing new words, much as the English language thrived and prospered in Shakespeare's day, when poets and playwrights vied in outshining each other with renderings of dazzling new words. The remarkable thing is that it works, and works very well. Despite the apparent anarchy surrounding its growth, modern Hebrew has emerged in a logical and stimulating pattern. It is almost never "bastardized." Even with the shoot-from-the-hip improvisations of amateur philologists and verbal face-liftings, there is a deep sense of continuity from biblical days. For example, the word for telegraph. *"Telegrama"* was used, but everyone detested it. Then someone thought of the wrath of Jehovah, and Jehovah's lightning, and *mivrak,* from the biblical word *barak,* lightning, filled the bill most pleasingly.

Because of this deliberate cultural atavism, as Professor Chaim Rabin of the Hebrew University has observed, modern Hebrew is not really distant from three-thousand-year-old biblical Hebrew. Modern English is light-years further from Chaucer, who is a mere half-thousand years away. The warnings, as most warnings against impossible dreams in Israel, have been proved wrong. "Hebrew is admirable for producing prophetic thunder, but you cannot play a scherzo on a ram's horn" it was predicted. "You cannot transform a Phoenician chariot, by fitting it out with borrowed spare parts, into a modern racing car" was another prediction.

Yea, verily, lo and behold, the ram's horn dances, and the Phoenician chariot races at dazzling speed. And it all began with the dreamer Ben Yehuda, who started with fumbling efforts, and whose best solution for "gloves" was "house for the hands," and who, when faced with inventing a word for "microscope," used the biblical phrase: "A glass by which the moss that springs out of the well shall grow like a cedar in Lebanon."

Comparison with other attempts to revive dormant languages are fascinating. As far as the present authors can establish, it has never occurred, in the history of the world, that an unspoken language was deliberately and successfully resurrected. Cornish, which had disappeared from spoken use for less than two hundred years, was revived with indifferent results. Gaelic and Lithuanian, both long suppressed, became official languages after World War I, but they had never ceased to be spoken in many homes and places of work. In the case of "emerging" nations with a heterogeneous population, the strongest ethnic group within the pioneer country usually imposed its language or dialect upon the others. Yiddish, therefore, the lingua franca of the central and eastern European Jews, should have won out in Israel; but the antipathy for everything Yiddish connoted ruled that out of the question. Years ago a nostalgic benefactor from abroad offered to fund a chair for Yiddish at the Hebrew University in Jerusalem; the offer was furiously refused. Lately, another offer was made for a chair in Yiddish and readily accepted. The danger of Yiddish as a competitive tongue has passed and Yiddish may be studied as a cultural phenomenon.

Israel's clock has been deliberately swung back to the sixth century B.C., when the poets, judges, and princes and farmers of Israel spoke Hebrew. But it is an electrical clock, functional rather than antique, and it runs briskly in the twentieth century. The ultimate accolade to Ben Yehuda's lifework, besides the Hebrew-speaking sabras, is the fact that today hate-filled, bloodcurdling programs from Radio Cairo and from Radio Ramallah in Jordan are beamed regularly toward Israeli listeners, in the tongue of the prophets—Hebrew.

CHAPTER IV

Experiment in Utopia

✡ "We shake off the old life which has grown rancid on us, and start from the beginning. We don't want to change, we don't want to improve. We want to begin from the beginning."
>
> —A. D. Gordon, spiritual father of the kibbutz movement

It is impossible ot understand the sabras without knowing the daring dreams of their fathers. Some sixty years ago, the elite of the early Zionists arriving in Palestine blueprinted a unique way of life called *kibbutz.* They wanted to create a new society based on mutual aid and brotherhood. They wanted to live nobly, and to rid themselves of greed, jealousy, and all else that was vile in man. They thrived in the desert, and no other factor in Israel today (always excepting the enmity of the Arabs) remotely approaches the shattering impact made by these bold idealists.

One example may suffice to show their immediacy even now. In 1910, ten starry-eyed boys and two girls from Poland emigrated to Palestine. Unable to find work, they decided to act out Utopia, to live and work together on a communal farm, and to share their money. They settled in a typhus- and malaria-ridden swamp, and theirs was the first kibbutz in

Palestine. One of them proposed that they take a stern vow not to marry for five years. "Living as we do," he said, "in this climate, in constant danger from the Arabs, how can we have children?" But a young girl from Russia joined the kibbutz, and within a few weeks a young man fell in love with her. They married, and one of their children is not unknown to the world. He is the sabra general Moshe Dayan.

*   *   *

Planning a better world has always been a harmless pastime of man, and the trouble begins only when he tries to live by his theories. The archaic yearning for a lost paradise is as old as the Greeks, and the history of Western thought is strewn with relics of the Golden Age, the Place of Harmony, the City of the Sun. They are synonymous with man's dream of happiness—the land of milk and honey.

Today we are weary and wary of utopias. The dreams of the nineteenth century became the nightmares of the twentieth. We are apprehensive of all schemes guaranteed to produce men like gods. Visions of an ideal future are unpopular. We don't want them. When vexed with our social ills, we find comfort in reading anti-utopias. It is difficult for us to believe that Edward Bellamy's *Looking Backward,* a novel presenting a smug Utopia, sold over two hundred thousand copies in the last century; our taste runs more to ominous "New Maps of Hell," such as *Brave New World* and *1984.* For pleasant fantasy we read science-fiction, rather than *Pictures of a Socialistic Future.*

Life where every detail is carefully regulated by a benevolent state fills us not with joy but with distress. So bitter has been our experience in our time that all visionaries are shrugged off. We do not wish sweeping reform of the way we live, but rather cautious compromise that will not rock the boat, nor blast us all to kingdom come. We have unwilling ears for anyone who has discovered the way to the New Jerusalem, where man will live in admirable decency. Our hopes are shabby: we have written off the hope of abolishing war, and seek but temporary delays from a new holocaust until we are safely removed from the scene. We bury our heads in technological races to the moon, while half the world starves.

Yet only a hundred years ago, and always before that, men vied with one another in confident vistas of the Good Place, where work would be attractive, private property condemned, and where proposals concerning sexual freedom would be heard with interest. At least they were not afraid to dream. After all, as Emerson remarked, what was man born for if not to be a reformer?

We reply, dream me no dreams, for every dream has its dark side. Plato (who would have scorned the idea of kibbutz) offered us a republic supported by the labor of slaves, which reeks to us today of fascism; in the Utopia of Thomas More, wars and executions were condoned; Karl Kautsky said that with Utopia modern socialism begins, but we have seen with our own eyes how it can lead to men becoming slaves of the state. It is safer to race to the moon.

*   *   *

The first kibbutzniks were Israel's founding fathers and early heroes. At the peak of its popularity, the kibbutz idea attracted never more than 12 per cent of the citizenry, and today less than one Israeli in twenty-five lives on a kibbutz. Yet the erect, righteous shadow of our Puritans still falls disapprovingly over all of us. Israel is obsessed with the kibbutz vision as America is still obsessed with the ethic of their Puritans—also fearless, elevated men who crossed an ocean and pioneered in the wilderness because of burning moral convictions.

But Israel's Puritans did not live over three hundred years ago—many of them are very much with us, alive and kicking, and their sabra children and grandchildren have grown up and reinforced their ranks. You cannot dwell in Israel today and escape their legacy. Even if you have no intention of going near a kibbutz, and instead seek a pleasant life in Tel Aviv, with a good job and a gracious home, and the ambitions, say, of people in Stockholm or Chicago, the kibbutzniks disturb you. They make you feel guilty. There they are, up in a lonely farm near the border, virtuously living a life of dedication. And here you are in Tel Aviv, chasing around in your selfish rat race. You secretly feel that if you were motivated enough, self-sacrificing enough, man enough, you'd chuck Tel Aviv and its fleshpots and toil in a flinty kibbutz and break your back.

The first kibbutzniks settled in the Jordan Valley, at the southern tip of Lake Tiberias. In the summer, this spot becomes a broiling tropical underworld with inhuman temperatures, and it seems perverse that the first commune of Palestine was set up in a steaming swamp. This swamp-desert was the cheapest land the Arab landlords were willing to sell. The kibbutzniks did not mind; they wanted life hard and challenging.

They called their new home Deganiah, "God's Wheat." Life was hell in this burning pesthole, and yet it was marvelously exciting. The average age of the group was twenty. They were like an extended family. They took their meals together in the communal dining hall, and bursting with youth and vitality, they talked and danced the hora and sang sad Russian songs until dawn. From the very beginning they worried whether or not their children would carry on their fantastic experiment of Utopia in the desert.

Palestine in 1910 was an almost barbaric land, an outpost of the corrupt and effete Turkish Empire. There were only about eighty thousand Jewish settlers in the country and most of these were pious Jews living on donations from abroad. The first Zionist villages had sprung up in the 1880's, but still less than one thousand families were engaged in farming. The bourgeoise Jewish farmers preferred to hire Arab labor, which could be had for low wages. Spurred by pogroms in Russia, between 1904 and 1914 some thirty-five thousand Jewish immigrants arrived, many of them inspired with the new ideal of a Jew working with his hands. There was simply no manual work for most of them, and many left the country. Others turned to the new kibbutz idea as a way out of their employment difficulties.

The example of the first communal farm, Deganiah, fascinated the new immigrants, as well as young Jews still in Europe. They became caught up with the dream of a New Jerusalem based on brotherhood, with no place for exploiters nor exploited, and far, far, from the wicked world.

Finding the world evil (especially evil for Jews), they withdrew into the desert to create a new little world. No one prophet's teachings satisfied them. They cross-planted Zionism with pure socialism, and with the gospels of Rousseau, Tolstoy, and Freud thrown in. They called their new way of life "ingathering," or kibbutz.

Today, there are more than two hundred kibbutzim prospering in Israel, and the early ones now possess a flourishing second and third generation, who are, of course, sabras. In sum, the kibbutz society has worked for more than half a century. You may not care to live your days in one of them, but you cannot deny that it is a daring advance toward a social utopia. It is the rare place where you can be born and later carried to your grave on a kibbutz hillside without ever having touched money.

The kibbutzim of Israel are perhaps the only free society in the world where individual property, by personal agreement, is invested in the community, thus creating a society where all men are economically equal (well, almost equal). This rural, arcadian communism has survived all trials without sacrificing its basic principles (well, not too many principles), and has welded its hopelessly naïve scheme into a subsidized but bustling concern.

These do-it-yourself farmer-intellectuals believed that man's noble human potential would flourish in a shared agrarian society where distinctions based on wealth, family, and power were unknown; where employing the labor of others was forbidden (this sacred principle caved in on most of the kibbutzim in the 1950's, because of the huge influx of new immigrants desperately needing jobs); where all physical labor in the community would be eagerly performed by the members themselves.

All this, of course, is preposterous. People do not live that way unless Big Brother is pointing a gun at their heads. (The Soviet Russians themselves admit their failure to communize their peasants.) At the beginning nothing could have seemed more lunatic, more wildly improbable. There was no one to guide the kibbutzniks in running Utopia, on a day-to-day basis. The only other Jews farming in Palestine were levantinized old settlers who employed Arabs, despised manual labor, and gave the daft pioneers a month before they fled.

The kibbutzniks were all alone in the Palestinian wasteland, a "land of corpses and graves, and Bedouin robbers, a land of malaria and eye diseases, a land which destroys its inhabitants." *

But in four thousand years of Jewish history, there is little without precedent. There were spiritual ancestors. A strikingly similar band of zealots, weary of the world and its ways, had gone forth into the Palestinian desert two thousand years be-

* Shlomo Zemach: *Introduction to the History of Labor Settlement in Palestine,* 1945.

fore. They too wished to shake off the old hateful life of the marketplace, and experimented with a visionary, communal life based on brotherhood. They called themselves the Children of Light; we know them as the Essenes, the people of the Dead Sea Scrolls.

*   *   *

✡ "They avoid the cities, because they well know the iniquities which have become inveterate among city dwellers . . . they stand almost alone in the whole of mankind because they have become moneyless, by deliberate action, rather than by lack of good fortune."

—Philo (First Century, A.D.)

Retreat to the desert is an ancient Jewish tradition, as old as Moses. Jewish prophets always sought out the desert, gave up family, home, and land, and searched for the face of God in the Wilderness.

There seems to be something in the uncompromising harshness of the desert that brings man face-to-face with spiritual realities. It offers no shade from the sun, or shelter from the night's cold. It is a life of extremes. Moral issues are as sharply defined as the patterns of light and shade on the bare rocks; sunlight and darkness, good and evil, God and Satan.*

About one hundred years before Christ, a band of idealists abandoned Jerusalem, the capital of the Jewish kingdom. They were disgusted with the corruption they beheld everywhere, and with the "seekers after smooth things." They were religious mystics. Except for a few scraps, the staggering library of scrolls they hid in their caves, when the Romans

* John Allegro, *The People of the Dead Sea Scrolls.* Doubleday, 1958.

were closing in on them, are the earliest Hebrew manuscripts we possess.

Pliny, who wrote in the first century A.D., has some tersely Roman words about them. On the western shore of the Dead Sea, the Essenes have withdrawn to a sufficient distance to avoid its noxious effects. A solitary people, and extraordinary beyond all others in the world . . . they live without money, having only the palms for companions.

In his famous book, *The Scrolls from the Dead Sea*, Edmund Wilson remarks:

In reading the contemporary accounts of the Essenes, we are struck by two kinds of resemblances. For one thing, the modern traveller is often reminded of the Israeli collective farms that are known as kibbutzim. Here the property is held in common, as that of the Essenes was; the purchasing is done by a manager or management. The members of these communities have in some cases even shared their wardrobe, putting on any clothes that would fit them, as the Essenes did their winter and summer cloaks. Like the Essenes, they bring up adopted children—in the case of the Israeli communities, orphans and children. They have had to face tyrants as terrible as any that the Essenes fled from, and it has given them the same sort of impulse toward natural brotherhood that inspired the monasteries of the Essenes.

There are many more intriguing similarities. Those who came to the Essene societies were vehement in their tirades against the dissolute Jews of the cities; the *chaverim*, or comrades, of the kibbutzim never tire of denouncing Tel Aviv as a modern Gomorrah. The Essenes were searching for moral certainty at a time when the old values of Judaism were being seduced by Greek ideas and civilization; the kibbutzim emerged at a time when Jews in western Europe and America were assimilating to a degree unheard of in all their long history. Both preached the beauty of the spirit and sought to overcome human greed and vanity.

There are among them no slaves and no masters. They maintain a fraternal equality, believing that human brotherhood is the natural relationship of man, which has only been destroyed in society by the competition of the covetous.

These are Philo's words on the Essenes. They may apply, verbatim, to the Israeli communes of the twentieth century.

A kibbutz is careful not to choose idlers, or neurotics; in the Essene communities it was not enough that a man should be momentarily dissatisfied with the world, for the severe discipline of life in the wilderness would break the will of any but the most convinced pilgrim. A kibbutznik must undergo a year's probation before he is accepted; with the Essenes, the trial period was usually three years. A new Essene member handed over to the overseer all his personal possessions; a new kibbutznik turns over his private wealth to the treasury of the settlement. Josephus tells us that the communal meals of the Essenes were preceded by ritual lustrations and a change of clothing; the kibbutz dining hall is the very core of kibbutz life, where the group spirit is stoutly maintained. The Sabbath and holiday meals on a kibbutz can be truly beautiful.

The Essenes loved learning, and the great library of scrolls they left us is astounding; they would gather in company to have the Scriptures read to them and expounded. The modern kibbutznik is anything but a country bumpkin; he is often an intellectual farmer, athirst for knowledge, and astonishingly well-informed on Sartre, Beckett, and, of course, world *politika*.

Both welcomed the purifying quality of a grim, ascetic life and self-denial. In the kibbutz today, as with the Essenes, "the sick are supported if they cannot work, and old people are cared for." (Pliny) "Everyone looks up to them as free by nature, and not subject to the frown of any human being," Philo writes in admiration. "There is no buying and selling between them. Not a single slave or servant exists among them, and the members have several occupations, at which, like rivals, they engage in with untiring energy, making neither heat nor cold a pretense or excuse." The devotion to labor is the cornerstone of kibbutz life.

It appears that some of the Essene communes accepted women, but reluctantly; most of them banned the sex. The presence of women was too distracting for those dedicated to the spirit, and the Essenes had renounced sexual desire. On the first kibbutzim there was a curious, determined de-emphasis of sex; everything from chastity to mixed showers was tried to cool the carnality of the flesh. To this day fancy clothes, cosmetics, and the like are often suspect on a kibbutz.

It is amazing how without women the Essenes proliferated from generation to generation; they did so by scouting for likely young men in the cities to replace their ranks, precisely as the modern kibbutz, not depending on marriage and natural increase alone, sends emissaries to all the towns and abroad, searching for "kibbutz material."

Above all, both yearned to scourge their souls of greed, anger, jealousy, lust, and all base motives. There is sometimes the aura of the saint about the kibbutznik, the man who has rid himself of the curse of materialism and fleshly pursuits. Today, when one beholds the inner peace, the serenity that is often found on the weather-beaten face of an old Israeli pioneer who has given forty years to his ideal, it is intensely moving.

It is curious that prior to the fairly recent discovery of the Scrolls, almost nothing was known or taught about Essenes in Israeli schools, where the heads of school children are stuffed with every wearisome phase of Jewish history. The reason for this seems to be the fact that the Essenes had broken away from Orthodox Judaism, and devoutly believed that they alone were the true remnant of Israel. Jewish religion has always been hostile to dissenters from its ranks and suspicious of false messiahs and prophets. After all, only fanatical adherence to their religion has kept the Jews alive as a people, despite pogroms and inquisitions.

There was another reason for Jewish reluctance to "accept" the Essenes. The discovery in our own time of the Scrolls has rocked both Judaism and Christendom; the Essenes appear to be an unexpected link between the two great religions.

To quote Professor Allegro:

Jesus of Nazareth was contemporary with one generation of Essenes. . . . Certainly the first Jewish Christians fell heir to ideas already believed and customs practised by the Essenes . . . The Scrolls are the source books out of which the New Testament emerged. They are an indispensable link between the Old Testament and the New.

On the Jewish side, Edmund Wilson observed, there is "a resistance to admitting that the religion of Jesus could have grown in an organic way, the product of a traceable sequence of pressures and inspirations." "As for the Christian side," Wilson notes, "one feels a certain nervousness, a reluctance to take hold of the subject and place it in historical perspective."

But today in Israel, especially with the sabras, the Essenes are revered. They are no longer skeletons in the closet, but famous ancestors and patron saints, and their Scrolls are handsomely enshrined in a special building in Jerusalem. Israelis, a nation of passionate amateur archeologists and historians, cannot hear enough about "these men no longer flooded by what is corporal, nor led astray by passion." A recent week-long seminar on the "People of the Scrolls" packed a large auditorium with young Israelis from all over the country, and the sessions began at eight-thirty every morning and ended at eleven in the evening. Every new unraveling of one of the many scrolls, which can take years, is followed by the nation at large with rapt interest.

We do not really know what became of the Essenes. They were almost certainly wiped out by the Romans in 66 A.D. in the great Jewish war against Rome. Before the eagles of the legions glinted in the harsh sunlight along the Dead Sea, the Essenes carefully hid their scriptures and hymns, their precious scrolls. They wrapped the manuscripts in linen and placed them in tall, wide-necked jars on the floor of cool, dry caves. No one lived again in this desolate corner of Palestine until new men appeared, more than eighteen hundred years later, men who, like the Essenes themselves, welcomed isolation and the whips and trials of the desert that cleansed the soul of its sickness; these men were the kibbutzniks.

Today the visitor with a feeling for history can walk freely through the ruins of the Essene's City of Salt, climb up the debris of stones to their tower, and brood, as he gazes across the Dead Sea, on the fate of these "Children of Light," as the Essenes called themselves when their walls were stormed at last by the Roman "Children of Darkness."

The visitor may also reflect on another Jewish war, that of June 1967, when the late Prime Minister of Israel, Levi Eshkol, was a member of a kibbutz; and when the Minister of Defense, Moshe Dayan, the son of kibbutzniks, in his eve-of-battle message to the Jewish troops, referred with humbleness to modern Israel as the new Children of Light.

*   *   *

America, the new-found land, the continent of Utopia, always made men dream; in the nineteenth century America teemed with ambitious ventures in communal living. Their leaders were not grand-scale reformers who sought to improve man's lot by political convulsions, but visionaries who sought fifty stout men, or even ten, to trek into the wilderness and build the New Jerusalem.

There were altogether more than 140 American villages and farms dedicated to Utopia, and more than one hundred thousand converts, from the beginning of the movement until its end. The societies were usually religious in character; marked by a yearning to return to the primitive Christianity practiced in the early centuries after Christ. They bore names like Harmony, Phalanx, Brook Farm, the Oneida Community, and were often led by a prophet with burning eyes and a penchant for meddling in the sex lives of his disciples. Each prophet was convinced that he alone had discovered the secrets of distribution of wealth, of happy marriages, of harmonious life in the Good Place, where man would be a little lower than the angels.

It is curious how close to the Jews the American reformers usually felt. They often called themselves Children of Israel; the Old Testament was always open at hand, and the guardian of the farm was always convinced that he was governing according to God's will. Some of them even gave their settlements Hebrew names, like *Adonai Shomo*. The Rappites in Pennsylvania preached that the Temple of Jerusalem was to be restored, and that the Twelve Tribes of Israel were to be re-established—a notion that had obsessed the puritan John Eliot, who labored mightily with the Indians, convinced that they were the lost tribes of Israel.

The Israeli kibbutzim are famous for their bold concepts of marriage and family (which, we believe, have done as much as anything else to hold them together), but there is little that has been tried in Israel, from "free" love to the communal rearing of children, that was not tried out by one or another of the American sects. The Americans experimented in sexuality with a will, from the Shakers who viewed both sex and marriages as evil, to the Oneida colony that tried group marriages and collective children's houses. This latter is a strikingly successful feature of kibbutz life today.

They all failed. Those American communes which survived into a second generation usually faltered with the indifference of the young, who had not gone through the white fire of conversion as had their elders. The communes are all vanished today, except for a few relics, footnotes to the quest for Utopia, charming signposts of half-forgotten Americana— Fruitlands, Nashoba, Economea, New Harmony, the Holy Hill of Zion, Icarie, Equality.

What went wrong? Why did the American schemes all whither away, usually to the jeers of their neighbors, while the palm trees of the kibbutzim in the Jordan Valley grow majestic in their second half-century of life? How have the Israeli pioneers succeeded in living in harmony with their fellow man?

The answer, we believe, lies in the Israeli kibbutznik's profound sense of building a new nation, and in his attitude toward work. On the American farms, work was always the great stumbling block. How to feed the Noble Savages? The members could never agree who was to do the boring manual labor that, alas! had to be done, and done daily. At New Harmony, they tried a time store, where one paid for goods in labor notes. At the North American Phalanx, and at Clarkson, it was decreed that the more disagreeable the labor, the more reward one would receive for it. None of these incentives helped; in most of the settlements, everyone demanded the right to short, not unpleasant, labor. This seems to have been their ruination.

The kibbutzniks solved this problem by not paying anybody, and by embracing a mystique that celebrated the virtue of the Jew laboring with his own hands in the soil of Palestine. This was preached by a remarkable Tolstoyan figure, A. D. Gordon. He was a frail man who in middle age came to Palestine, unknown and unannounced, and began at once to labor in the fields by the side of the far younger comrades.

Gordon became their spiritual leader, with his "idea of the spade." Revered in his lifetime, since his death he remains a legend. It was he who preached the gospel that fired the imagination of young Jews, of land-roots, of the healing, restoring effects upon the Jew, locked for centuries in ghettos and cities, who again toils his ancient land himself. Today, at Kibbutz Deganiah, there is a little museum of Gordon memorabilia, and mention of Gordon's creed, *"dat avodah,"* the mystic worship of labor which ennobles, often brings skeptical looks from the third-generation sabras of Deganiah, stolid farmers' sons for whom Deganiah is home and work is work.

*   *   *

Why so much talk about kibbutz when today less than 4 per cent of Israelis live on them?

The kibbutzim belongs to Israel's neo-Rousseauistic past, really; the army takes care of defense now, not the man with the plow and the rifle (although the rifleman still defends his farm against sudden attacks and often dies doing so). Instead of a few pioneers striking out for themselves, urban planners blueprint whole towns in the desert. The kibbutzim are in sad decline as Israel grows, and their role diminishes in a technological era. Their downfall was spelled in the 1950's, really, when Jewish immigrants from Arab lands (who form the majority of immigrants today) began arriving. These newcomers despised manual labor as an affront to masculine dignity, and went straight to the towns and cities.

Nevertheless, the kibbutzim have taken the brunt of the terrorist raids; in 1968, a week did not pass that a children's dormitory was not shelled or a farmer wounded or killed when his tractor ran over a mine. In the north, on the Golan Heights, where the Syrians used to have their bunkers and artillery, paramilitary kibbutzim have been set up by young boy and girl soldiers, and youngsters from abroad. (These dangerous frontier posts have always attracted volunteers.) For this reason alone, the kibbutzim are anything but a luxury.

There is another reason why we respect and honor them: the kibbutz movement has been of far greater importance than its numbers would suggest. Their settlements were the vanguard of the state itself. They have provided the elite of the nation. Two prime ministers, Ben-Gurion and Levi Eshkol, have both been *chaverim,* comrades of a kibbutz. So are the men mentioned as future prime ministers. Many of the present cabinet, and about a third of the *Knesset* (Israel's Parliament) are at least nominal members of a kibbutz. The army has many kibbutz officers and in the Six Days' War, their contribution was enormous: among other things, kibbutz fatalities accounted for 24 per cent of the total killed in action.

In sum, they are the flower of our sabras, and speak and act for the best qualities of the nation. As J. L. Talmon has written, "If there ever was a ruling elite, and moreover one not based upon wealth, this is it." Also, the kibbutzniks are modern Israel's "Jews," in a wry sense—a proud, gifted, irrational, intractable minority, "the other society," and they often make everyone else feel uncomfortable.

The kibbutzim gave Israel its unique character as a social experiment. They are a national heritage of gallant men and women who were not afraid to dream of the Good Place where man would live with his brother in brotherhood. With all their shortcomings, they are the most admirable, the most successful, voluntary socialism since the communes of early Christians in the earlier centuries after Christ.

The Sabras of World War I:
The Nili Spies

✡ "We will go and make contact with the British, the enemy. If the Turks catch us, they'll sentence us as spies. Good. They'll hang us. Good. Even if the whole Yishuv [Jewish community of Palestine] suffers for this, we must do it. . . . Don't you feel a new generation is born? Don't you feel it coming?"

—Absalom Feinberg

"I employed as spies some 15 Jews from Palestine, all of splendid physique, and to my astonishment, fair-haired and blue-eyed. They worked in a team. Their leader was Aaron Aaronsohn, a man who feared nothing and had an immense intellect. I am not at liberty to divulge most of their exploits as it would publicize methods better kept secret."

—"Middle East Diary" (Yoseloff, New York) by Colonel Richard Meinertzhagen, British Army, on the Staff of General Allenby in World War I, and later Military Adviser to the Middle East Department of the British Foreign Office.

In the sleepy village of Zichron Yaakov, which winds amidst olive groves and vineyards high along Mount Carmel, there is a strange and beautiful house. Well-kept palm trees line its approach, and everything inside is always dusted, but the visitor at once feels something unreal and shrouded about this place.

This is the Aaronsohn home. Nothing in the living room has been changed for half a century. There are yellowed pictures of Sarah and of her brother Aaron on the walls. Aaron's beloved collection of stones and minerals are under glass, and old letters lie on the old-fashioned Turkish coffee table.

The Aaronsohns are legendary in Israel. They had much of the enigmatic qualities of the Brontës in England. Talented, aloof, disdainful, they were resented, even hated. During World War I they organized the pro-British underground band known as the Nili Spies. Palestine at that time was an outpost of the Turkish Empire. The savage Turks were allies of Germany, and at war with England. The wild hope of Nili, to win Palestine for the British, and in return win British support for a Jewish Palestine, seemed madness itself.

When Eliazer Ben Yehuda's first modern Hebrew dictionary appeared, in 1904, among the many letters of congratulation received was one from a fourteen-year-old sabra named Sarah Aaronsohn. She told the revered master how excited she was about his dictionary, and proudly added that her family also endeavored, in their modest way, to make Hebrew a living language. She confessed that "none of the children in our village knew the names of the flowers and the plants in their own language, as children of other nations knew theirs," but with the help of the new Hebrew dictionary they hoped to learn. The eager girl's letter rushed on, and she wrote about her adored brother Aaron, "who makes journeys all over our beautiful land, and always comes back laden with plants and stones. He strokes them, and guards them as though they were pearls, and writes all their names down on a nice card."

Thirteen years later Sarah, bleeding from blows, had shot

herself in the bathroom of her home, after vicious torture by the Turks, who wanted the names of her comrades in the espionage ring; her brother Aaron later vanished in a small British Army plane over the English Channel; Zvi Aaronsohn, another brother, was tortured and remained an incurable invalid; among their associates the sabra Absalom Feinberg, dressed as an Arab, had been killed in the sands of Sinai while trying to make contact with British Intelligence in Egypt; Reuven Schwartz was hung by his jailors from the bars of his prison cell in Nazareth; Yosef Lishansky was hung in chains in Damascus, shouting from the gallows, "Long live the English redeemers!"

These were the Nili Spies—a tiny band of Palestinian Jews who risked their lives throughout World War I to achieve an end that seemed at the time utterly fantastic: the overthrow of the barbaric Turks and the welcoming of the benign power of England.

Why did they put their wits against the Turkish Empire, and against fifty thousand German soldiers who were in Palestine as Turkey's ally? Because they were fired with the utterly implausible vision of a Jewish state in Palestine. Absalom Feinberg, their romantic, impetuous dreamer wrote, "I would set fire to the Turks as one lights a candle, if it would achieve our aim.

The story of the Nili Spies is virtually unknown outside of Israel. You will find no mention of them whatever in most books relating the history of modern Palestine.

Ironically, in Jerusalem and Tel Aviv, where there is not one obscure figure in Jewish history who does not have a street named after him, you will find almost no reminder of the Nili Group. Until recently, school-children in Israel barely heard their name. Zionist annals gave them only terse mention. So high does passion about them still run in the 1960's, a radio program about the Nili Spies was canceled at the personal insistence of Rachel Ben Zvi, widow of a late president of Israel.

Nili's allies, the British, have always known the valuable work that the Nili group did. An official veil of silence, however, was drawn about them after World War I. Britain was courting the Arabs frantically, and was not interested in praising Jewish-Palestinian aid to the allies.

But some British military men spoke up after World War I, and gratefully acknowledged the efforts of Nili. One was Lt. General G. M. Macdonough, Head of Military Intelligence at the British War Office from 1916 to 1919. In a lecture at the Royal Military Academy at Woolich in 1921 he declared, "English Intelligence was victorious in 1918. You will no doubt remember the great campaign of Lord Allenby in Palestine that year, and perhaps you are surprised at the daring of his action when he conquered Jerusalem. The truth is that Allenby took no unwarranted risks. He knew for certainty from intelligence in Palestine of all the preparations, and of all the movements of his Turkish enemy. All the cards of his enemy had been revealed to him, and he could play his hand with complete confidence."

Turkey, in World War I, had thrown in her lot on the side of the Germans, and Palestine, critically close to the Suez Canal, was part of the Turkish Empire. Allenby's "intelligence in Palestine" was the Jewish group called Nili. This was confirmed by Captain Raymond Savage, Deputy Military Secretary to Field-Marshall Allenby, who told the New York press in 1924:

"It was very largely the daring work of young spies, most of them natives of Palestine, which enabled the Field-Marshal to accomplish his undertaking so effectively. The leader of the spy system was a young Jewess, a Miss Sarah Aaronsohn."

Yet, in Palestine, where bitter memories die hard, the Nili

Group—until their "rehabilitation" in 1967—was a pariah, cursed as madmen and adventurers, and excommunicated with black candles in synagogues. They endangered the life of every Jew living in Palestine under the cruel Turks, and this, for Nili's neighbors, was unforgiveable.

There were, however, always some who did not abhor Nili, but loved them deeply, and who still weep over Sarah and Absalom and their brave comrades. Hundreds of girls in Israel today have been given the first name "Nili," in defiant remembrance.

It is time to tell their story.

* * *

Sarah's parents had come to Palestine from Roumania in 1882. They were refused permission to land and were tossed from port to port for forty days. The Sultan of Turkey had become suspicious of the first Zionists, and was sure they represented a British plot to seize Palestine. Disraeli just seven years before had bought up the Suez Canal shares, and the Turks felt the British lion eyeing their empire hungrily.

The Aaronsohns bribed their way to land—everything was possible with baksheesh under the Turks—and settled at Zichron Yaakov, near Haifa, a filthy disease-laden hamlet with a half-dozen wretched Arab huts. Their six children, with the exception of the oldest son, Aaron, were all born there. By the time Sarah was born there were a hundred Jewish families in Zichron. Like the Brontës in England, the Aaronsohn brood grew up devoted to each other and to the lonely grandeur of their countryside.

What is more, even though they grew up at the turn of the century, they were already "sabras to the core." That is, they never regarded themselves as merely children of Jewish parents who happened to be living in a malarial outpost of the Ottoman Empire. Rather, they read the Bible avidly and loved the epic of ancient Jewish glory. They felt themselves proud heirs to all this and dreamed of a Hebrew-speaking nation reborn.

Aaron, the oldest of the children, from all accounts was a remarkable man. He was a naturalist and botanist of phenomenal intellect, and found more than three thousand varieties of plants in Palestine. His discovery of wild wheat made him world-famous among agriculturalists. He was a large man, proud, arrogant, and instantly aroused the fury of those he treated as his inferiors; and yet the American diplomat William C. Bullitt wrote of him, "Aaron seemed a sort of giant of an elder day—like Prometheus. He was the quintessence of life: torrential, prodigal, and joyous. He was the greatest man I have ever known."

Sarah herself was a high-spirited girl with the firm strength of the traditional Jewish matriarch, and was much loved by men throughout her short, tragic life. A close friend of Aaron's and Sarah's great love, was Absalom Feinberg, a passionate, strikingly handsome young sabra with a romantic, melancholic nature. Absalom was a poet and a crack horseman, respected by the Arabs for his fearless riding.

The Aaronsohns in time became fairly comfortable plantation owners, employed cheap Arab labor, and despised the Russian and Polish intellectual Jews who began streaming into Palestine after the abortive 1905 revolution in Russia. The older settlers pinned their hopes on Theodor Herzl's political maneuvers, and on the Charter from the Turkish Sultan that he was always on the verge of receiving. They called these newcomers "The Barefoot-Ones," and laughed at their socialist credo that Jews must work the land themselves. One of the "Barefoot-Ones" was an indomitable young man named David Ben-Gurion, who fought the entrenched planters tooth and nail for the next forty years.

There was a "little sister" among the Aaronsohn brood,

Rivka; Absalom became infatuated with her, and after a while it was understood that the couple were engaged. Jewish tradition as old as Rachel and Jacob forbade the marriage, as long as an elder sister in the family remained unmarried; Sarah stepped out of her younger sister's way by accepting a loveless match with a Jewish businessman in Turkey. She went to live in Constantinople, a dim Oriental style menage with latticed windows for the restricted women. Absalom, in the manner of fond young men, realized at once with her absence that it was Sarah he really loved, and began writing her passionate letters. Six weeks later, World War I broke out.

*   *   *

Turkey, saturated with German advisers and money for a generation, entered the war on the side of Germany. The Aaronsohns, like everyone else in Palestine, assumed that it was only a matter of weeks before the British occupied Palestine, if only to safeguard the Suez Canal, which Britain then held. There was almost nothing to stop the British from coming through the desert of Sinai, or landing anywhere on the coast by ship. There was no Turkish artillery in Palestine, there were no planes, and the coastal defense was in the hands of a wretched Arab militia. Had the British landed, they would have unquestionably been received with open arms by the local population of Mohammedans, Druse, Christians, and Jews, for whom life under the Turks was insufferable.

But the British had no intention of invading Palestine, and Winston Churchill's plea for "this obvious maneuver" was dismissed as "venturesome and impractical."

The Aarohnsohns waited impatiently, intending to put themselves at the disposal of the British the moment they landed. They knew that this would be the heaven-sent chance to unite their own hopes for freedom with British interest in the Middle East, even though official Zionism still maintained its headquarters in Berlin, and assumed that Jewish fate in Palestine was inevitably locked with Turkey's own destiny.

Life for the Yishuv (the Jewish community) became more and more intolerable as the war progressed. The Turkish army vandalized Palestine, carrying off all food for the front. Near starvation was common in the towns. News of the Turkish activities against the Armenians seeped into Palestine; a whole people were being deported and wiped out. A Turkish "specialist in Zionist affairs" arrived in Palestine, declared the Jews foreigners and traitors, and mass expulsion of Jews began. Men, women, and children were rounded up without warning from their homes in Jaffa and taken to the port without even being allowed to make contact with their families. The Turks were happily using the war as a pretext to rid themselves of their despised non-Muslim minorities, Jews and Christians alike.

The person in charge of the terror was Djemal Pasha, the Chief of the Fourth Army, a squat, almost hunchbacked man with terrible black eyes. Djemal began jailing and exiling Jews and Christians from the moment he arrived in Palestine. All Jews were ordered to hand over whatever weapons they had. The Aaronsohns, who had a cache of arms which they used to defend their village from Arab raids, refused. Alex Aaronsohn, another brother, was imprisoned; he revealed the whereabouts of their weapons only when the Turks advised him that they would round up all the young girls of Zichron and hand them over to the Turkish officers.

The war dragged on, with no sign of the British moving toward Palestine. In 1915 came the incredible news that the British had landed instead at Galipoli. They had decided to pit their strength against the Dardanelles straits of Turkey. Their plan was, in Churchill's words, (Churchill was First Sea Lord in the British Cabinet) "to open the Dardanelles and enable the Anglo-Greek Fleet to fight and sink the Turk-

German ships. From there, the whole situation can be dominated, in combination with the Black Sea Fleet of the Russians and their military forces." *

Aaron and Sarah and their circle of friends were thunderstruck. They could only conclude that the much admired British Intelligence had no idea what was going on within the Ottoman Empire. Aaron decided to take the fate of the Yishuv into his own hands, and somehow to contact the British in Egypt, and tell them how easily they could take Palestine. He would also offer the services of the Aaronsohns and their friends as spies behind enemy lines, even though they knew that if the Turks found out, their vengeance on the Yishuv would be terrible, and perhaps mean the end of any Jewish future in Palestine.

The risks were tremendous, and Aaron was aware of them. As he later wrote, "I decided to convince the British that it is in their own interest to attack Palestine immediately. If I had left the country and openly taken service on the British side, that would have been bad enough. But I did worse. I stayed where I was. I organized a whole movement connected with British Intelligence. I do not like mincing words. Put it clearly and say I became a spy."

But how to establish contact with the British High Command in Egypt? It was not so simple. One way was across the Sinai desert, which was covered by Turkish patrols. That was bad enough, but far worse was the fear of thirst. "And thirst," as Absalom put it, "is an enemy that is hard to conquer." Across the open Mediterranean to Egypt even in a sailing skiff was a simple matter, but the French had launched a vigilant blockade of the Syrian-Palestinian coast, and shot every boat of any description at sight.

The group decided to send Alex Aaronsohn, who was

* Winston Churchill, *The World Crisis*, Vol. 1.

twenty-seven, tall, very sure of himself, and bound to make a favorable impression upon the British. Using a forged Spanish passport, Alex got out in June on the American warship *Des Moines,* which had called to take to Egypt persons expelled from Palestine. (America was still neutral in the war.) In Cairo, Alex had the shock of being met with indifference, even hostility, by the British High Command. Most of the officers to whom Alex talked had no idea that there were any Jews living in Palestine. He was suspected of being a Turkish agent. Besides, the British stationed in Egypt were solely interested in guarding the Canal, and had no interest in Palestine. As for underminding the Turks, T. E. Lawrence and the Arab Bureau were busy with schemes of fostering new Arab rulers who would be a threat to Turkish power and later prove loyal friends of Britain. Alex went on to America, to do propaganda work for the Jews of Palestine, who were nearly starving.

Back at Zichron, Aaron and Absalom waited tensely for news from Alex, but heard nothing, as no mail could arrive. Absalom was in a frenzy of impatience. He meant business. Even as a student of seventeen in France, he had written, "I am prepared to die even tomorrow, and alone, to achieve the Jewish revival." He despised the majority of Jews in Palestine who were terrified of incurring the wrath of the Turks. "Our worst enemy is the Turk," he wrote. "Now that the hour of his downfall has struck, can we stand by and do nothing? If the time has come for us to die, we'll die."

The American ship *Des Moines* reappeared in Haifa, Absalom boarded it with a false Russian passport and got to Egypt. He had better luck than Alex had had; at Port Said he was put in touch with a Lieutenant Woolsey of Naval Intelligence, who was impressed with the story of the young Palestinian Jew. Woolsey was not in a position to discuss the armed uprising that Absalom sketched out, but agreed to use the Zichron group for intelligence. A British patrol passed along the coast of Palestine from time to time and would call at Athlit, the beach below the cliffs on Zichron, whenever signaled.

Jauntily, Absalom returned home on a small French warship, and was rowed ashore at Athlit. As though returning from a gay holiday, he gave presents to all the family and advised Aaron that contact had been made. "Lt. Woolsey is that rarity among the English," he said. "He has intuition. He can sense things." In another ten days a ship would pass, and Absalom, signaling from shore with a cigarette, would be met by a sailor who would collect whatever information they had prepared for His Majesty's Forces.

No sailor came. The ship arrived, signaled in a confusing way, and steamed off. Aaron and Absalom lay all night on the beach at Athlit, with a leather pouch crammed with information on Turkish troop strength and arms movements. They could see the patrol ship cross and recross Athlit, but they could not decipher its messages. Later, they learned that the British had suddenly changed their signaling code.

On tenterhooks, and sensing that something had gone wrong, Absalom decided to get to Port Said again. Lt. Woolsey must be disappointed, he thought. "I don't want the Commander to think that the first young Jew in his service betrayed him."

There was no way out by sea now; Absalom was ready, despite Aaron's hesitations, to try to get through overland across the Sinai desert, through the Turkish front. He set off on horseback, was caught by a Turkish patrol only a few miles before Suez, and was thrown into prison at Beersheba, to be hung as a spy. Through feverish activity by Aaron, who was an adviser to Djemal Pasha on the locust plague and agricultural matters, Absalom was released after three weeks.

He returned light-heartedly to Zichron and found Sarah there.

Lonely in Constantinople, with mail from Palestine cut off, Sarah had decided to return home. She had left her husband and traveled a month through wartime Turkey. Rivka, her younger sister for whose sake she had given up Absalom, had been packed off to America for the duration. The lovers were together. Sarah without hesitation, even enthusiastically, joined the amateur spy ring. Shortly afterwards, British Intelligence in Egypt began to hear of a vast Turkish build-up in the Sinai desert. According to their reports, it sounded as though Turkey and Germany were concentrating for an attack on the Suez Canal. Lieutenant Woolsey decided once again to try to contact the Jewish group at Zichron, and found a Palestinian who knew the area.

One dark night at Athlit, in the shadow of the old Crusader castle, a man swam to shore, and left a note on a plow on the beach. A worker found it and brought it to Aaron. It was from Lieutenant Woolsey. He wrote that in three weeks' time a ship would pass again and they should contact it, according to the code he supplied now.

The conspirators were overjoyed, but the ship never came. It was torpedoed en route, and Lieutenant Woolsey was taken prisoner. He spent the rest of the war in a camp in Turkey.

What to do now? Aaron set out for Constantinople, hoping to get to Britain through a complicated route across neutral Copenhagen. Absalom and Sarah remained in Zichron, restless and frustrated. Life at Zichron was stark; the Turks had taken all the crops, and meals consisted largely of tea made out of fig leaves with bread made of coarse Arab barley.

Absalom, always impetuous, struck out once more for Egypt, this time again across Sinai. Sarah tried to stop him, but she knew she could not. She had had a premonition that Absalom would inevitably die trying to contact the British.

He left a note for Lieutenant Woolsey, in case the patrol ship would suddenly appear in his absence, "I have decided, come what may, to cross the desert and to reach you. I must run my last race, and I beg you to note that I do this in the service of His Majesty, George V, King of England, who, in my mind, is already crowned King of Palestine and Mesopotamia. . . ."

Absalom set out with another of the group, Yosef Lishansky, a cocky, vain, and unstable member who loved danger as much as he loved the notion of a Jewish Palestine. Dressed as Bedouins, they had started off by camel from Beersheba, and took the precaution of hiring a Bedouin guide.

Sarah was left in charge of gathering information about the Turkish Army. This work went on all the time.

In the meantime, Aaron had gotten to neutral Copenhagen from Constantinople, and went from there to London. He was arrested as an enemy alien who was probably a spy and handed over to Scotland Yard. They turned him over to the War Office, who sent him on to Cairo to tell once more his fantastic story of a band of Jews behind enemy lines in Palestine, who were willing to risk their lives, without pay, to help the British cause.

In Cairo, his words fell on deaf ears. The High Command was not stirred by the proposal of large-scale revolt in Palestine, and just could not believe that *Jews* could be of any military value, in the improbable event that the story happened to be true. Aaron lingered in Cairo, bitter and furious with the British, and then through luck his story reached the ears of Brigadier General (Sir) Gilbert Clayton, who knew the Middle East upside down. Clayton felt a ring of truth in Aaron's fantastic tale, and turned him over to his right-hand man, Major Wyndham Deedes, an expert in Turkish affairs. Major Deedes immediately ordered that measures should be taken to renew contact with the Zichron group.

One reason for General Clayton's interest in Palestinian

spies was the fact that the Gallipoli expedition had not gone as cheerily as planned. Churchill had declared, "A good army of 50,000 men and sea-power—that is the end of the Turkish menace." * Instead, there were a quarter of a million Allied casualties, in return for three small footholds.

Aaron was elated by Major Deedes's action. He remained in Cairo and made sure that contact would really be kept up this time. His one worry was what rash scheme the impulsive Absalom might have gotten himself into during Aaron's absence. On January 25 a Captain Edwards was waiting for Aaron at his hotel. Edwards told him, "I've been looking for you since this morning. You must go at once to Port Said. One of your men has reached there through the desert."

Stunned, Aaron knew it could only be Absalom. He hurried to Port Said and found there, severely wounded, Yosef Lishansky, the man who had gone with Absalom on the dangerous journey across Sinai. Lishansky told him that he and Absalom had almost reached the no-man's-land between the Turkish and British lines at Suez, when a band of thirty Bedouins had surrounded them. A battle broke out, and Lishanksy had been wounded in the neck. Absalom had fought off the Bedouins as long as he could, but was struck down when his bullets were gone. He was dead, his body still lying in the sands of the desert. Lishansky, alone, without water or camels, and bleeding to death, had crawled painfully through the desert until he had met a British patrol.

*   *   *

Back in Zichron, Sarah pined for news which never came. Alex and Rivka were in America; she had no way of hearing from Aaron, who was behind enemy lines in Egypt. She was in agony over the fate of Absalom, and could not rest until she would see his striking face once more.

* Churchill, *The World Crisis*, Vol. 1.

One night a man appeared "half-demented, looking with startled eyes at his surroundings, stammering unintelligible words. The smell of alcohol was on his breath, and he was trembling from shock, and dripping water at every step." * He fumbled in his pocket, and handed Sarah a medallion she had given to Aaron before he had left Palestine.

The stranger told her that he had been rowed ashore from the *Monegam*, which now was anchored just beyond Athlit. Aaron was on the ship but dared not come ashore to see her for fear of being recognized. What about Absalom? The man did not know.

Sarah handed him a leather pouch crammed with reports. She yearned to run to the seashore, to shout to the ship for news of Absalom, but she knew it was madness, and would endanger them all. Aaron asked that Liova Bornstein, one of the devoted members of the group, come join him in Egypt for a while. Liova, nearly drowning, swam out to where the boatmen were waiting for him. The *Monegam* slipped away in the moonless night, and the next night anchored again off Athlit. This time, Yosef Lishansky, who had gone with Absalom, was rowed ashore. He told Sarah that Absalom was dead. From that moment she closed accounts with life; the eager, gay young woman who had been Sarah died with Absalom, and she now lived only to complete Absalom's work. "To continue what my dear one began—that is all I wish," she wrote to Aaron. "And vengeance, great vengeance, on the wild ones of the desert, and on the cruel Turk. May God only give us life to continue."

The *Monegam* at once set sail for Egypt. Aaron told Liova what had happened to Absalom, and the two friends sat miserably on deck all night, barely speaking.

Liova sat with his Bible in his lap—a gift from Absalom.

* From the unpublished memoirs of Liova Schneersohn.

One of the Intelligence officers came up to where the two men were huddled and began chatting. He told them he was from New Zealand, and yearning to be home.

"By the way," he said to Aaron," what's your password?"

Aaron looked at him blankly.

"You've got to have a password, you know," the New Zealander said. "For your spy organization. A code word that we use as the name of your group."

Aaron shrugged, and turned to Liova. "What name shall we use?"

Liova turned to his Bible, and it fell open at 1 Samuel XV. The sentence read, "The Eternity of Israel will not lie." It was spoken by Samuel, the priest, to King Saul, after Samuel had declared to Saul, "The Lord Hath rent the kingdom of Israel from this day, and hath given it to a neighbor of thine, that is better than thou."

It is a practice among Jews who love the Bible to form names from the initials of crucial or momentous passages from the Bible. In Hebrew this sentence "The eternity of Israel will not lie," reads "Netzach Israel Lo Ishakare."

"That's our password," Liova said. "Nili," pronouncing it in Hebrew, *Neelee.*

"Nellie?" chuckled the New Zealander, "That's a nice name. The Nellie spies."

*   *   *

Sarah threw herself into the work, now that the British urgently awaited reports from Nili. Turkish and German troop movements, the food situation, locations of arms dumps —everything was noted in the leather pouch. To be effective, it was necessary to expand the ring, and Sarah sought new recruits. She approached an old friend of the family, Dr. Neumann, who was now chief military doctor for the Turkish forces stationed at Affulah. Dr. Neumann's duties included inspecting trainloads of soldiers as they arrived. This was a vital junction, and a fine place to gather information, because all men and supplies from Constantinople and Damascus streamed through Affulah on their way to the Turkish front in Suez.

Sarah handed him a note from Aaron, appealing to Dr. Neumann to join the Nili spies. He read the letter and flung it aside. "I'll be risking my head if I do this madness!" he cried to Sarah.

She answered quietly, "You see, Doctor, my own head sits firmly on my shoulders, but I am risking it every day. If you are a man, you will do the same." Neumann joined Nili, and did valuable work.

Sarah and Yosef Lishanksy visited Jerusalem, and learned the vital news that the Germans already had fifty thousand soldiers in the country, under General von Kressenstein. From one of their contacts, they received a map of Jerusalem with all German fortifications marked on it. They also warned the British that the Bedouin tribes, selling oranges to British troops along the Suez Canal, were really spies for the Turks.

*   *   *

The *Monegam* appeared regularly now at Athlit, and Sarah and the others risked death by waiting for it on the seashore, under the noses of Turkish soldiers all through the area.

Liova, or another of the group, would be rowed ashore, the reports would be handed to him, and Sarah would receive letters, new instructions, and newspapers from Aaron. Few words were spoken; every moment the ship loitered near shore made the danger greater. The pouches were exchanged —*Shalom!*—and the visitors from the sea immediately turned back to their little boat that rowed to the *Monegam*. Several times Arabs, hearing suspicious sounds on the beach, fired upon them; once a caravan of twenty camels plodded past the sand while Sarah crouched, hidden in the darkness. A German U-boat began prowling the coast and Nili's agents reported that the U-boat was searching for a British ship that came regularly to the area.

It was impossible to conceal entirely from other Jews in the area the existence of Nili. Rumors spread throughout the Yishuv that a few Jews were carrying on espionage for the British and preparing the way for armed uprising against the Turks. All the official leaders of the Yishuv were enraged. They had struggled all through the war to assure the Turks that the Jews were loyal. They knew that if the Turks discovered a spy ring of Jews within Palestine, their vengeance would be swift and terrible upon all Jews in the Yishuv, not just upon the handful of spies.

As the word of Nili spread, Sarah was beset by implacable Jewish foes on every side. She was urged that only by complete loyalty to the Turks could the Yishuv hope to survive with the war. Later would be the time for political negotiations, and if the British won, well and good. Within Zichron itself, it was painful for her to be told by neighbors and old friends that if she were caught in her mad scheme they would all be tortured and hung. She knew it to be true. but could not help herself.

Her own brother, Zvi, begged her to quit. She heard again and again, "Who can say for sure that the British will succeed? And if they do, will they get here before the Turks kill us all when they find out what you are doing?"

The leaders of *Hashomer,* the official Jewish home defense militia of the time, decided that Nili must be broken up. It was officially agreed that Sarah and her comrades be kidnapped, taken away under guard, and forbidden to appear at any point near the coast.

But two weeks later, Djemal Pasha, the Turkish commander in Palestine, ordered the expulsion of all Jews from

Jaffa and from its new sister-town, Tel-Aviv. The British had captured Bagdad, and attacked Gaza, the first indication of a large allied offensive against Palestine. Djamal Pasha signed the expulsion order and declared, "I know that the Jews in Palestine await the British like a bride awaits her bridegroom, but as the bridegroom comes closer, we will remove the bride farther away."

The Yishuv's plans to smash Nili were forgotten with this new blow that affected everyone. They waited in dread for further persecutions from Djemal Pasha and they soon came. Plans were announced to expel the Jews of Jerusalem to the desert of Transjordan. There they would surely die of starvatoin, as did the Armenians when expelled by the Turks to the Syrian desert.

The *Monegam* arrived regularly, and on one voyage to Athlit brought Sarah some carrier pigeons. She had no idea what they were for until she opened the letters from Aaron. He wrote jubilantly that the British had a new general, Allenby, and things were humming. Allenby had met Aaron, liked him, and had deluged him with questions about malaria, the waterless desert, and all the myriad problems that Allenby would face with his army in the unknown desert that loomed before them on the road to conquest of Jerusalem.

The carrier pigeons were to dispatch information from Sarah and her Nili group to Allenby's headquarters in Wadi Gaza within hours. Allenby was planning a surprise attack on the Beersheba front. A long list of questions was enclosed regarding Turkish strength in that section, the replies to which were to be sent at once via the pigeons.

Sarah answered, and added, "We've heard that they are preparing a list of 100 names, and we head the list. They (the Yishuv) intended handing over the list to the Turks if the Jews are threatened again, and say, 'here are the people who have been engaged in this foul work. . . .' How true all this is I don't know, but they could do a thing like that, couldn't they?"

The espionage work picked up tempo, and Sarah and Lishanksy traveled all over Palestine. The carrier pigeons were a headache. They had been trained badly; when the first were sent to El Arish, one returned in two days with the code message in the cylinder still strapped to his leg. The pigeon had apparently just been wandering about the neighborhood, jeopardizing all their lives. The next pigeon they sent was no better, and Sarah dared not send any more. The Turks were not exactly efficient, but the German army was everywhere now.

Things were looking up, however. The British attack for which she longed seemed to be imminent, a matter of weeks only, perhaps less. Besides, Aaron wrote happily from Cairo, *mirabile dictu,* the British Government would soon come out publicly in favor of a Jewish national home in Palestine. The High Command in Cairo had been instructed to send "Major Aaron Aaronsohn" to London for special consultations in regard to this momentous decision. There was more heady news. A Jewish fighting force was being mobilized in England and in America for the liberation of Palestine. This had been Absalom's dream from the beginning.

The work of Nili seemed to be drawing to a close. Aaron urged Sarah to come to Cairo now. She was able to think of the day when the work would be over and mission accomplished. "Peace! A British-governed Palestine! I don't know how I will get used to it, without the troubles, and without the work," she wrote to Aaron.

While they were writing letters of future plans, the day-to-day espionage went on. Sarah was using the pigeons again, although terrified by their unpredictability. But as the British were able to bomb German troop concentrations near

Beersheba within hours after Sarah had alerted them via carrier pigeon, she went on with them regardless.

On September 3, Sarah dispatched several pigeons with messages. The same afternoon, she noticed one of them still hovering over the beach. Her stomach turning over with dread, she threw a pebble at it, and it flew off. The next day word reached Nili that a carrier pigeon had been caught by the Turks. It had been found at Caesaria, not far along the sea from Athlit. The Moudir, the Arab police chief there, had been feeding his own pigeons, and noticed that one was a stranger. He glanced at it more closely and saw the little cylinder with a coded message attached to its leg.

*   *   *

The Turkish officer in charge of finding the espionage ring was Hassan Bey, the Kaimakam (governor) of Haifa. Hassan Bey was a gentle-looking man, a hashish addict, and a notorious sadist who enjoyed watching the tortures he inflicted. He methodically began tracking down the espionage ring and had already searched Hadera and Caesaria, towns not far from Zichron. He had not turned up anything but then he became lucky. Naaman Belkind, one of the Nili spies, against Sarah's orders, and without telling anyone, had set out across Sinai to solve the mystery of Absalom's disappearance. (Sarah and Aaron had never revealed Absalom's death in Sinai because that would have at once aroused suspicion that he had been trying to reach the British.) Naaman had been captured, given drugged wine, and revealed much about Nili.

Sarah and Yosef killed all the pigeons and frantically buried all papers and documents. On October 4 Hassan Bey arrived in Zichron with his special squad of soldiers who had had experience in torture among the Armenians. He threatened to leave no house standing unless he was given the name of everyone connected with the Jewish spy ring. They tortured a half-dozen men, then put Sarah in chains and led her across the village. They tortured her for three days, but she refused to tell them anything.

"Beat me as much as you want," she taunted them. "You won't get anything out of me. You think that because I'm a woman I'll be weak. I despise you. I despise you and death. Hit! Torture me! I will be avenged, your end is near."

Those listening to her cries nearly went mad. Others of the village, who hated Nili, ran through the streets shouting and rejoicing vindictively, and fell upon each new Jewish victim the Turks carried off, beating and abusing them as they were dragged through the village. The Turks took Sarah to the house that had been Aaron's office. Unable to get any word out of her, they tortured her seventy-year-old father, and her brother Zvi, to make her crack. On the third day they decided to remove Sarah and the others to Turkish Headquarters at Nazareth, where the interrogations would continue under the supervision of the infamous Hassan Bek, Chief Medical Officer of the Turkish Fourth Army. Sarah asked permission to go home and change her blood-soaked clothes before the journey.

Bound with chains, she stumbled through the streets of Zichron for the last time. Every person in the village watched her from behind shuttered windows. Before the tall palm trees of her father's house, she rested for a moment and gazed about her at the street where she had lived most of her life. Then she entered the house, and the guard remained outside while she went into the bathroom. She wrote a letter to Aaron, "I haven't the strength to suffer anymore. The tortures are something terrible. It was terrible seeing my father suffer so. I've been given the most murderous beatings. They chained me with iron chains. Remember to tell of our suffering to those who are coming. . . ."

Sarah took a pistol she had hidden in the bathroom and

shot herself in the mouth. The bullet passed through her tongue and lodged in her spine, leaving her arms and legs paralyzed. She was in terrible agony for another three days, and was frightened she was going mad from the pain. She kept moaning and pleading for someone to kill her, and after three days she died. She was not yet twenty-seven.

Three nights later, the *Monegam* appeared once more off the coast near Zichron, followed by two warships of the British Navy. They had received word that the Nili group had been betrayed, and had come to rescue Sarah, despite the risks for all concerned. They lowered two small boats and rowed ashore, but at the cave that was their usual rendezvouz point with Nili, no one was there to greet them.

Alex, Sarah's brother, had come on the ship, and he wandered about the shore, together with Captain Weldon, the British officer in charge. A cold wind roared up, and above the wind they whispered, "Nili! Nili!"

They stood there a moment, dreading the silence. Receiving no signal, they dared not trudge inland, but could not bring themselves to turn their backs and row out to the waiting ship without Sarah and the others of Nili. They waited on the shore for an hour, then signaled the little boat to come and fetch them. Alex was sunk in despair, could not speak as the cold waves splashed about them. In his pocket he had brought a present for Sarah. It was a telegram from Dr. Chaim Weitzmann, who was in London, and was some thirty years later to become the first president of the state of Israel. The telegram read: "We are doing our best to make sure Palestine Jewish under British protection. Your heroic stand encourages our efforts. Be strong and of good courage until the redemption of Israel. Weitzmann."

In December, General Allenby conquered Jerusalem.

*　　　　　*　　　　　*

Exactly half a century after Sarah killed herself, Nili was somewhat "rehabilitated" by the state of Israel. Absalom's grave in Sinai had been found and identified after the Six Days' War, and his remains were transferred for burial on Mount Herzl in Jerusalem, the resting place of Israel's greats.

It was a solemn, military ceremony, although not a state funeral—the President of Israel did not attend, but sent his aide-de-camp. Many other old-timers, now members of Knesset, refused to pay their respects. Passion and bitterness about the right or wrong of Nili is still common in Israel, and undercurrents of suspicion and hostility still smoldered at the ceremony itself. There has always been a grimly vindictive streak among the Jews against their own dissidents; nothing, no one, can be allowed to interfere with the course of the Ship of Zion. This trait runs from the time of Moses, who cried unto the Lord, "What shall I do unto this people, they be almost ready to stone me?" to the wrath of the orthodox against the Essenes, the people of the Dead Sea Scrolls; in modern times the deadly hatred of the majority for Nili was repeated thirty years later against the stern gang terrorists who were fighting the British. When Premier Levi Eshkol died in 1969, David Ben-Gurion, who felt that Eshkol turned against him, refused to attend the funeral of his old comrade.

And yet the Jews are not alone in castigating the visionary, the rebel who with his defiance risks the heads of all about him. The implacable opposition of many Americans to the revolutionists against England in 1776 is well known. During the Easter Uprising in Ireland in 1916, people pushed against the soldiers who guarded captured rebels, and spat against their fellow Irish who had brought havoc to the citizenry. Time softens these hard memories, and the despised agitator becomes the scowling old-fashioned personage whose picture hangs on schoolroom walls.

At Absalom's funeral bier, the eulogy was read by the

Speaker of the Knesset, Kadish Luz, who had been one of the "Barefoot Ones" on a kibbutz himself. Luz spoke of the "tragic misunderstandings with which Jewish history is so rich," and attributed the conflict between Nili and the Yishuv to a startling reason. "The conflict," he said, "was brought about by the arrogance of the sabra members of Nili. The native born young took no pains to conceal their feelings that they were superior, that they were capable of assuming and coping with greater responsibility than other Jews."

This is an intriguing explanation, and points to the fact that members of the generation of Nili's time were "the first sabras," fully equipped with the sabra traits discussed in this book—pride, arrogance, an impatient desire for action, and a profound sense of Jewish nationalism. They were the first green shoots breaking through the petrified forest that Jews had lived in for eighteen hundred years. They proved how natural the instinct for freedom would be for Jews born in their own land, not tolerated strangers in a foreign land. Sarah and Absalom and Aaron and the others were the prototypes of the dauntless sabras who thirty years later, in Israel's War of Independence, fought the first of three wars to defend their liberty. Nili was the spark of the flame.

Absalom Feinberg personified the sabra *par excellence*. At the age of twelve he had already organized a group of his school chums to work for a Jewish state. Brooding, headstrong, romantic, poetic, arrogant, brave, sabras today love the memory of Absalom as the very essence of all the new qualities that are treasured in Israel. Not for nothing has he been called "The Sabra Heathcliffe."

Absalom was also very much utterly at home in the lonely Levant—a striking quality of today's sabras. "You cannot understand the beauties of the East," he once wrote, "but I am a Jew of the East. I can understand the mystery, the beauty, the gaiety of the East. The hot nights in summer, the windy nights in winter. I hear the song of the Bedouin, the song he sings on his night watch, and it says much more to me than the music of your Wagner and your Beethoven.

"Get away from me, you cold man of the north. We'll show the world what our people can do. I don't mean the miserable ones from Berdichev and Mohilev, (Poland) but we, from the land of Israel, the new ones, the unknown until now. The proud Jews, the braves ones, the ones whose hearts are not eaten by the Galuth (foreign soil). Don't you feel a new generation is born? Don't you hear it coming?"

The Speaker of the Knesset, eulogizing Absalom, went on to say that it is hard for us today to understand the background to the bitterness and ill-feeling that made Nili a pariah for so many years. "Only now, with the perspective of half a century, we can appreciate how daring their movement had been. . . . Our presence here in united Jerusalem is in some measure thanks to their sacrifice."

But just what did Nili accomplish? It is difficult to estimate. Nili's dream of an uprising against the Turks never came about, and the British would have taken Palestine without Nili. Nevertheless, the Jewish spies unquestionably made their trek through the desert far easier and less bloody, and proved the valor and loyalty of the Palestinian Jews.

Official British historians of World War I pass over Nili in silence. Nili were foreign spies, something always rather abhorrent, and as Aaron once remarked gloomily, "I don't see Britain showering honors on spies." Besides, Britain after the war was ecstatically praising the efforts of Lawrence of Arabia and his exploits among the Arabs, who were also groaning under the Turks.*

* There is a still-lively school of romanticizers who believe that Sarah Aaronsohn was the "S.A." to whom T. E. Lawrence's book, *Seven Pillars of Wisdom* is dedicated. This notion is based on the fact that Lawrence, as a subaltern, visited Athlit before the war, and studied the Crusader castle there. It is claimed that Lawrence met Sarah at Zichron, and fell in love with the

Despite the Balfour Declaration, Britain's military men on the scene in the Middle East were aghast at the idea of Jews streaming into Palestine. General Allenby refused to allow the Balfour Declaration to be announced in Jerusalem, and was in no mood to arouse Arab resentment further with praise of a Jewish spy ring that had helped to win Palestine.

Still, that famous letter known as the Balfour Declaration would have warmed Sarah and Absalom. On November 2, 1917, the British War Cabinet issued the Balfour Declaration in which "His Majesty's Government view with favor the establishment in Palestine of a national home for the Jewish people. . . ." This was an infuriatingly unclear document "which allowed Britain to acquire the Holy Land with a good conscience," in Barbara Tuchman's words.

But it is probably just as well that the Nili Spies did not live to claim their reward from a grateful Britain. They would have clearly expected to be repaid with the leadership of a Jewish Palestine. Aaron Aaronsohn certainly hoped for

---

young Jewess whose ambitions were as daring and romantic as his own. In 1938, the London Daily Express headlined a story "Woman in Lawrence of Arabia's Life was A Spy," and went on . . . "She was Sarah Aaronsohn, a red-haired Jewess, who was head of the British Secret Service in Palestine. While still in her 20's she shot herself when tortured by the Turks. Whether they were lovers probably no one will ever know."

In December 29, 1956, the London Journal *New Statesman* carried a letter from a Mr. Douglas Duff, who declared that Lawrence himself told him that *Seven Pillars* had been dedicated to Sarah Aaronsohn. Duff had recently himself written a book on Palestine, and had dedicated it to Sarah. He quotes the following conversation between Lawrence and himself, at a chance meeting:

Lawrence: "Did you know Sarah Aaronsohn while she was alive?"
Duff: "I'm very sorry that I did not. I'd have given my arm to have done so."
Lawrence: "Why?'
Duff: "Good Lord, man, if ever there was a Joan of Arc in our days, it was Sarah!"
Lawrence: "Strange, we two men should be here in this little town, both of us with a book dedicated to Sarah, without either of us having ever seen her alive. We were partners, Sarah and I, but without meeting. . . ."
Duff relates that he met Lawrence some weeks later, and the latter told him then, "If Sarah had had a man for a husband, she might have been the leader of a Hebrew return to glory."

this reward. He had been directing Nili liaison from Cairo, and had escaped the fate of his comrades in Palestine, who were all tracked down and arrested.* In 1917 he spent much time in London with the British statesmen who were mulling over the Balfour Declaration. He fully expected, in return for the work of Nili, to become the officially recognized instrument through which Britain would direct its benevolent efforts toward the Jews.

But Britain was uncomfortable with this spy, this flaming, turbulent man of action, and much preferred to negotiate with the orthodox Ship of Zion, the proper representatives of world Jewery, and the moderate, safe Dr. Weitzmann, a man who was "almost frighteningly convincing," as Sir Ronald Storrs remarked.

Aaron stayed on in London, bitter, broken, shunned as a heretic by the proper Zionists. He hoped to be useful at the Peace Conference in Paris. In 1918, he boarded a small British Army plane, together with all documents concerning Nili, and flew toward Paris. A heavy fog rose over the Channel, and the plane bearing Aaron Aaronsohn, the leader of the Nili spies, vanished in the mists.

* After the war, Alex Aaronsohn hunted down the dreaded Turkish torturer, Hassan Bek, who had directed the interrogations against the Nili members in Nazareth, after Sarah's death. Alex found him in Aleppo. Hassan Bek was brought to trial in Jerusalem and sentenced to long years of hard labor for the death of Reuven Schwartz, one of the Nili group. Hassan Bek was released a few months after Alex's plea, "Vengeance is the Lord's." Following his release, Hassan Bek was struck with paralysis and never walked for the rest of his life.

CHAPTER VI

A Sentimental Education

✡ "Ireland, they say, has the honor of being the only country which
has never persecuted the Jews. Do you know why?
   "Why, sir?" Stephen asked.
   "Because she never let them in," Mr. Deasy said solemnly.
                                                    —James Joyce, *Ulysses*

It is the custom in Israel for married couples to dine on Friday night with the parents of the wife or of the husband. In
a certain Tel Aviv family—we'll call them Joel and Miriam—
they go to Joel's mother every Friday without fail. They invariably return home wan and emotionally spent.

There are two sturdy sabra grandchildren who make the
table gay. Miriam is pleasant and obedient toward her
mother-in-law, and Joel appears to be relaxed and enjoying
his Sabbath eve. The talk is lively, and an outsider would
think that all this chitchat flowed naturally. But the truth is
that the tension around the table is electric. Joel and Miriam
strive desperately to keep the conversation away from *politika*, and from any reminiscence of what went on in this
hectic country a quarter of a century ago, when Israel was
still Palestine, and ruled by the British. If anything at all
reminds Joel's mother of those stormy days, her face contorts

and she snaps at her grandchildren, or she tells Miriam that she is spending too much money on food.

But she is really saying silently to her son, flinging at him, "The man who stayed alive! A coward I nursed at my breast. God, I'm ashamed to look at you."

This sounds crazy unless you know Israeli *politika,* and what we call *ahavat moledet,* love of the motherland. It is pure fanaticism, of course, but Israel was forged in fire by implacable fanatics, honor-student terrorists, and resurrected Maccabees. Across the centuries, more blood has been shed for Palestine than for any scrap of land on earth. The Holy Land has not been the ideal place to train law-abiding citizens.

Chana, Joel's mother, is a women of sixty with still-blazing eyes and a lantern jaw and a face like a creased map. As a young girl in Poland, she, with her husband, had become intoxicated with the new wine of Zionism. The mystic longing of the Jews for Palestine had been transformed into a legal claim with the Balfour Declaration, and the League of Nations Mandate to Britain; the official promise of a national home, encouraged thousands of young idealists. Chana's parents, whom she adored, were violently opposed to their daughter emigrating to the far-off desert of Palestine. Why should a nice Jewish girl want to leave civilized Poland, with its three and a half million Jews?

But there is no arguing with headstrong youth. Chana and her husband bribed their way to Turkey, trudged on foot through Syria and Lebanon, and crawled, more dead than alive, into The Land. The year was 1923. Three years later Chana gave birth to a son, Joel. A month later Chana's husband was killed in an Arab riot in the Jewish quarter of Jaffa.

Chana was alone with her baby. She lived in a shanty along the seashore, and with a little cart and donkey, supported herself by selling milk in the streets. Joel helped her, even as a toddler. Chana liked having him around her all the time, and besides, there was no one else to look after the child. He was all she had, and Chana loved the boy dearly. She told him stories, not very accurate, of the fighting heroes of Israel—Judas the Maccabee, "The Hammer," the deliverer of Judah against the Seleucid Greeks; Eliazar Ben Yair, the Commander at Masada; Joseph Trumpeldor, the one-armed pioneer who died in Galilee in 1920. Together with fifty young men and women, Trumpeldor's band held four besieged kibbutzim for two months before being overwhelmed by the Arabs.

Ten dramatic years went by, the national home prospered, and beginning in 1933 there was a sudden influx of many Jews fleeing from Hitler's Germany. Their tragedy became the dynamo of Jewish development in Palestine, and the sad illustration of the more than ever urgent need for a Jewish land.

Then it was 1939, and Joel was ten years old and looked just like his dead father. Chana hoped that Joel would be a scientist when he grew up, and she was already putting away a few pounds for the tuition fees he would need at the Hebrew University.

The year 1939 was a fateful one for all people—World War II began. For the Jews of Palestine, the year was even more ominous; the Nazis "final solution" began—nothing less than the extermination of the Jews. And in that black year, the British Government under Mr. Chamberlain announced its White Paper, which slammed the door on further immigration of Jews to Palestine.

As with the relating of any personal story of someone who lives in Israel, we must pause in Chana and Joel's narrative, and explain the *politika* of the period. For the British Government under Neville Chamberlain, the Jews of Palestine were a nuisance. The British Cabinet in 1917 had proclaimed its gallant Balfour Declaration, and thereupon rashly became the sponsors of a romantic adventure with the Jews that the

British Foreign Office abhorred and did not know how to get out of. The oil-rich Arabs of the Middle East were a mighty force to be constantly wooed and appeased; fed up at last with their unfortunate promise to the Jews, Britain made a complete about-face. The half million Jews in Palestine were written off with proper murmurs of condolences. Neville Chamberlain was the architect of the Munich Pact, which abandoned Czechoslovakia to Hitler; he was hardly the man to risk the wrath of forty million Arabs, and the possibility of an Arab Holy War, to honor that maddening, unclear, and thoroughly regrettable solemn pledge to the Jews, the Balfour Declaration.

Following this determined new policy as declared in its White Paper, Britain from 1939 until 1948 threw up a formidable blockade around the shores of Palestine. A flotilla of the British Navy month after month prevented the wretched Jewish refugees of Europe from reaching the country. Not one nation in the world wanted the hundreds of thousands of Jews (except in token numbers) who had somehow escaped the Nazis; most of the Jews were doomed as the German war machine raced across Europe. Refused visas to Palestine, turned back if they somehow managed to reach there, six million Jews perished in the crematoria of Buchenwald and Auschwitz.

For the Jews of Palestine, the White Paper was another Munich, and a catastrophe. It limited further Jewish immigration to seventy-five thousand over a period of five years, and made all Jewish settlements after 1944 "subject to Arab approval," and it prohibited, in effect, the sale of land by Arabs to Jews. It spelled the end of the Zionist adventure; in the words of Winston Churchill, it trapped the Jews of Palestine in "one more precarious oriental ghetto." *

* Debate on the White Paper in the House of Commons, May 1939.

For Chana, as for all her neighbors, the White Paper was more than a new political twist: it was a personal tragedy. They had all left behind in Europe parents and brothers and sisters, who were now certain to die a vicious death at the hands of the Germans. For a year before World War II broke out, Chana had been trying frantically to get her parents out of Poland. She learned they had escaped to Hungary. She had actually secured passage for them; then the British announced that no Palestinian visas whatever would be granted to "persons coming from Germany or German-held Poland." Chana heard that her father had been taken to Buchenwald concentration camp. She had no idea what had happened to her mother.

For all the six black years of World War II, Chana did not know whether her parents were alive or dead, nor what had happened to everyone else she had loved back in Poland. It was a long nightmare of dread for her. This sustained suspense and fear is difficult to describe; it molded a community of raging, desperate people.

In April 1939, three refugee ships, the *Assandu,* the *Assimi,* and the *Panagia Konstario,* laden with half-dead Jews who had somehow escaped from Germany and Roumania, reached the shores of Palestine. The British refused permission to land and declared them to be illegal immigrants. The refugees were turned back to their port of origin, even though it could mean sending them back to the German New Order.

For the tense Jews of Palestine, this was war. Ben-Gurion declared then in a famous remark: "We shall fight with Great Britain in this war as if there were no White Paper. And we shall fight the White Paper as if there were no war."

For the British, it was also a little war, within the framework of the World War; for almost a decade they were to become obsessed with hunting down the little death-ships. On September 1, 1939, the first two refugees were killed on board the immigrant-packed ship, *Tiger Hill,* when a British Police coastal cutter opened fire.

Questions were raised in the House of Commons. "This is the breach, this is the violation of the pledge, this is the abandonment of the Balfour Declaration," roared the old lion, Winston Churchill, "this is the end of the vision, of the hope, of the dream." *

In 1940, a seventy-five-foot sailing boat, the *Salvador,* reached Turkey, with 350 Jewish refugees from Bulgaria aboard. The *Salvador* was turned back to the high seas. A violent storm broke out, and 231 men, women, and children were drowned as the boat smashed to bits. Some of the survivors were sent back to Bulgaria, which was under German occupation.

One day a woman came to see Chana. The visitor was a refugee herself, and had swum to shore, unseen by the British, from one of the ships that had arrived. The stranger reported that Chana's mother had reached Turkey, and would soon arrive in Palestine, on the illegal immigrant ship, the *Pacific.*

Chana was overwhelmed with emotion. She rapidly made plans for taking care of her mother, and she scrubbed her shack and prepared enough food for a family of ten. She bought a new bed, and fixed the leaking roof. Trembling with excitement, she could not sleep until the *Pacific* arrived. By British ruling, anyone in Palestine harboring an "illegal" immigrant, even his own father or mother, was liable to an eight-year prison sentence (the penalty for harboring a murderer was only three years), but Chana did not worry about that.

In November 1940, two battered tramp steamers, the *Pacific* and the *Milos* arrived in Haifa port with eighteen

---

* Commons Debate on the White Paper, May 23, 1939.

hundred Jews. Several hundreds of them had families already living in Palestine, as did Chana's mother.

Chana and her son Joel were waiting in Haifa for two days before the *Pacific* was due. Hundreds of other people were also in Haifa, to meet their relatives on the eagerly expected ships.

The *Pacific* and the *Milos* were not allowed to disembark passengers. A British warship surrounded them. Then the announcement came that the passengers would be sent to the island of Mauritius for the duration of the war. They were transferred, screaming and protesting, to the British steamer *Patria*. Like Chana, everyone watching on shore was refused permission to speak a few words to their loved ones.

On the day the *Patria* was scheduled to sail, November 25, 1940, the passengers blew up the ship. More than two hundred of them were blown to bits, or drowned within the safe haven of Haifa Port, as their relatives, including Chana, and just about the entire population of Haifa, watched with horrified eyes.

Among those who saw the *Patria* explode was a fourteen-year-old boy named Eliahu Ben Hakim. Standing on Mount Carmel, high about the lovely panorama of Haifa, he raised his binoculars and observed the thrashing bodies drowning in the water, and women without heads or legs being dragged into the boats by fishhooks. Four years later, in Cairo, this boy shot Lord Moyne, Britain's highest official in the Middle East. Ben Hakim was hanged. It was Lord Moyne who had cried, when told of a Jewish plan to barter from Hitler's Eichman a million Jews in return for trucks, "My dear fellow, whatever shall I do with a million Jews?"

Chana never saw her mother; the old woman was one of those blown to bits in Haifa Port. But when Chana's son Joel said he was joining the terrorist, anti-British, anti-Arab "National Military Organization," the *Irgun,* Chana only nodded her head.

       *   *   *

Around 1935, some young firebrands had formed a clandestine group with the grandiloquent title "Irgun Z'vai Leumi," the National Army Organization. The Irgun took orders only from its own leaders and despised the Haganah order of the day, "Your duty is to beat off attacks, but not to let the smell of blood go to your heads." The Irgun had no objection to the smell of blood. Swift retaliation and terrorism made up its grim philosophy.

In 1939, when Arabs had attacked Jewish civilians, Irgun boys and girls in reprisal hurled bombs into the teeming Arab quarters of all the large towns of Palestine. Scores of Arabs were killed. Most of the Jewish citizenry reeled back in horror; this was the first large-scale terrorist action by Jews. Never before in modern Palestine had Jews retaliated the wanton murder of their own people with equally wanton murder.

Haganah, the moderate, disciplined, self-defense militia of Palestine Jews, published a bitter leaflet, attacking Irgun with the biblical commandment: "Thou shalt not kill." The secret radio of the Irgun replied with Exodus 23-25: "Life for life, eye for eye, tooth for tooth, hand for hand, burning for burning."

The agony of the little death-ships swelled the terrorist ranks. The Irgun was a tiny band then, and without the new, unbearable spectacle of Jews drowning within sight of Palestine, it is doubtful whether the terrorism would have burgeoned into a serious force. The British, for many Jews, became overnight more than the occupying force of Palestine; they became deadly enemies.

With the outbreak of World War II, an uneasy truce was

concluded between the British and two Jewish undergrounds, Haganah and Irgun. After all, His Majesty's Forces were leading the struggle against Hitler, the most dread enemy the Jews had faced in four thousand years. The argument of the rebels over how much or how little violence should be used against the British, to force them to admit Jews to Palestine, was reluctantly shelved for the duration.

But a small group of students within the Irgun refused to go along with the "truce" and formed yet a third underground band. They felt as did David Friedman-Yellin, who wrote that his "mother and three brothers had been killed by German sadism and the British White Paper." Friedman-Yellin, a science graduate, later became the head of the terrorist Stern Gang. One of the leaders of the new terrorist band was Avraham Stern, a young student at the Hebrew University and a fanatical gunman-poet. Stern wrote poems like "Let our blood be a red carpet on the streets," and he was a poet who lived what he wrote. He denounced the truce and left the Irgun, taking with him other young men and women who were convinced that only unrestricted and indiscriminate terror would get the Jews into, and the British out of, Palestine.

They came to be known in the headlines of the world press as "The Stern Gang," or, more honorably, "Fighters for the Freedom of Israel." The Stern Gang derided Haganah's proud self-restraint as what would be called today Uncle Tomism. (The comparisons here with the various black American protest groups of the 1960's are fascinating, by the way.) The Stern Gang regarded the Irgun's truce with the British as quixotic. The Irgun had made a nice distinction in their etiquette of terror, blowing up British installations, and so on, but avoiding the killing of British personnel. The Stern Gang, however, had no such hesitations.

In the hot summer of 1939, the leaders of Irgun were arrested by the British, and some of them (according to the Irgun) were tortured by a certain Police Inspector Cairns. Irgun struck back by passing its own death sentence on Cairns, which it announced by secret radio to the British. Despite every precaution, Cairns and another police officer were killed by an Irgun bomb in August 1939.

This event rocked the Jews of Palestine. It was the first anti-British terrorist action by the Irgun. Later, Avraham Stern was mowed down by the British on the roof of an old house in Tel Aviv.

* * *

Until her mother's death on the *Patria*, Chana had been shocked by the terrorists. Nice Jewish boys behaving like Cossacks, and throwing bombs! Shooting with guns, instead of studying! But now she saw no other way. The Irgun was dangerous, and she dreaded to think that Joel might be killed on one of their missions, but she was convinced of their ruthless reasoning.

Joel, all of sixteen, was a harmless-looking boy with dreamy eyes. He played his shepherd's flute alone on the seashore, wrote poetry, and was crazy about a girl named Miriam. He guardedly told Miriam that he was joining the Irgun, and she kissed him for the first time and said she loved him because he was a hero.

The next two years were happy ones for Joel. He almost flunked his Irgun initiation under a brilliant spotlight, when they asked him questions and he only stuttered, but the high command of the Irgun decided that he was obedient and would be good material. Along with other recruits. Joel marched, learned to take a revolver apart and to put it together again while blindfolded, sang songs about ancient Jewish heroes, and recited poems like "In blood and fire did

Judea fall, in blood and fire will Judea rise again." In a
blacked-out cellar they studied revolts of other people against
the British, and the Irish rebels sent them plenty of literature
and advice.

It was a fine time. Joel had to work during the day to earn
a living, but work and food and money meant nothing. At
night he planned hold-ups on British banks, or actions against
British Army camps to get arms for his comrades. Joel knew
that arrest and torture were always real dangers, but he felt
alive, and life had rich meaning and purpose.

The little ships kept coming. Ironically—the history of this
era seethes with ironies—the show of naked British force,
rather than frightening off the Jewish refugees, hardened
their determination. Their will to reach Palestine was
stronger than the White Paper. Three days before the Jews
aboard the *Patria* had blown up the ship rather than leave
Palestine, the paddle-ship *Atlantic* had lurched into Haifa,
carrying 1880 survivors of the Jewish community of Danzig
among its sad cargo. Typhus had broken out, and in the last
twelve hours fifteen passengers had died on board. Palestine
Jews were still fishing for corpses from the *Patria* while British officials were busy taking off the new arrivals from the
Atlantic—by force, as the naked and hysterical Jews of the
Atlantic fought back. These new refugees were sent to
Mauritius. They were kept there for five years, until August
1945. During the first two and a half years the male deportees
were held in prison cells; the women lived in corrugated-iron
huts, twenty-four to a hut. They were permitted to see each
other three times a week for two hours. Ten per cent of the
deportees died of tropical diseases; fifty children were born
on the island.

The most harrowing chapter in this list of "stupid, callous,
and inhuman acts" (Lord Davies in the House of Lords on

March 11, 1942) was the story of the sinking of the *Struma*. There is no Israeli veteran settler of today for whom the *Struma* tragedy is not a searing, unforgettable memory; there is no sabra school child who has not learned its details. On September 16, 1941, an 180-ton cattleboat, the *Struma*, entered the harbor of Istanbul. The ship was in unseaworthy condition; 769 passengers were herded into cages on a deck measuring 60 × 20 feet. Many of them were on the verge of insanity. The *Struma* remained in Istanbul port for over five months, while Jewish leaders in Jerusalem pleaded desperately with the British authorities for Palestinian visas. The request was refused. On February 24, the Turkish officials, fed up, sent the vessel back to the Black Sea. The fate of the *Patria* was repeated; within a mile of the Turkish coast, the *Struma* sank with its entire load of passengers, including two hundred fifty women and seventy children. There was one survivor.

A few days after the *Struma* tragedy, Irgun posters appeared on the walls of every town in Palestine. They were printed in Hebrew and English, and showed a photograph of the British High Commissioner for Palestine. The text below read:

MURDER
Sir Harold MacMichael, known as High Commissioner of Palestine, wanted for the murder by drowning of 800 refugees aboard the *Struma*.

"Jewish terrorism had started in Earnest," Arthur Koestler wrote. "It had grown out of the terror of the sea, the gaping mouths of the drowning, the deaf-mute gesture of their splashing hands. The drifting corpses gave blood—poisoning to the nation. The measured utterances of officialdom were answered by the rattle of the automatics of fanatical gunmen.

Lawlessness had become the supreme law of the Holy Land." *

With the end of World War II in 1945, the Irgun quickly stepped up its activity. Joel served with bravery in actions that dynamited British railways, and fough it out with British soldiers. He knew that the Irgun must win. Britain had to keep a hundred thousand soldiers in Palestine, just to repress the Jewish terrorists. It was costing Britain a fortune, eighty million pounds in two years, which they could ill afford since the war. Sooner or later, they would have to reverse their hated policy of forbidding Jews to come to Palestine. They might even be forced to abandon Palestine itself.

All hell was breaking loose in Palestine now. In each of the major cities, Jerusalem, Tel Aviv, and Haifa, the fearful British surrounded themselves against terrorists in high-walled, permanently guarded "security zones," which the Jews at once dubbed "Bevingrads."

In late 1946 a seventeen-year-old Irgun "soldier" was tried by a military court for carrying arms. He was sentenced to eighteen years imprisonment—eighteen lashes were added to the sentence.

The Irgun—in ultimatums headlined around the world by enthusiastic press correspondents—warned Britain not to carry out the beating. On the eve of the Sabbath, Binyamin Kimhi, the Irgun boy, was flogged.

Two days later, Irgun units captured two British officers, gave them each eighteen lashes, and sent them back to their unit.

As the perceptive Shmuel Katz wrote, "This simple physical and symbolic act made manifest the significance and implica-

* Arthur Koestler, "Promise and Fulfillment (1949). Koestler's historical account, and his novel, "Thieves in the Night," are indispensable for anyone who wants to understand the shaping of life in Israel. Koestler himself was a member of a kibbutz for some years. Both his books were heavily attacked in Israel, and remain unsurpassed for their penetrating insight.

tions of British rule in Palestine and the essence of the Jewish revolt. Even in Britain chagrin was mingled with wry understanding of the Irgun reprisal. Britain got the point, and a sentence of flogging passed on a second Irgun boy was abruptly canceled. (They even canceled a scheduled flogging on a rebel in India.)

Chana's hair turned white, but she never begged her son to quit. Then he was caught in a raid on a British Army camp, in which two British soldiers were wounded. Together with three Irgun comrades, Joel was brought to trial before a British judge. The British, who had had their courtrooms turned into public debating rooms by previous Jewish terrorists, announced that any Irgun prisoner who refused to accept a lawyer, and the usual trial proceedings, would be summarily hanged. From previous cases, the Irgun boys knew that if they submitted to the trial, and asked for "The King's Clemency," they could expect to get five to ten years in jail.

In the teeth of this, the Irgun ordered the prisoners to refuse to participate in the trial, and to challenge the authority of Britishers to try a Jew of Palestine. The British were foreign usurpers, declared the Irgun, and only a Jewish state could judge Jews.

Journalists from thirty countries crowded into the tiny courtroom, and it was a golden opportunity for Irgun to show the world that Palestinian Jews were more than ready to die for freedom.

Joel was in agony. He was twenty, very much in love with Miriam, and he wanted to live forever. It was all very well to risk being shot down in spectacular Irgun raids, but to step coolly onto the gallows was another matter. He sounded out Miriam, when she came to see him in jail, and he learned, with interest, that she preferred him alive, too.

His mother came to see him. Chana walked in gravely, looking much aged; besides Joel's capture, she had recently heard through the Red Cross that her father had died in Buchenwald camp. She was dressed in black, and her eyes were dry. She pressed her son to her bosom and gave him some chicken soup to keep his morale up during the British trial.

"You're all I have," she said. "I won't be able to live through this myself."

Joel's stomach turned over as he realized that his mother expected him to hang. He turned away, and could not look at her. As she prepared to leave, he stammered out that he was going to appeal for The King's Clemency. Chana stiffened as though struck, and then burst into tears. When the guard entered the cell to lead her out, she was still sobbing. She did not visit him again.

As the trial approached, all Palestine spoke of nothing else. Chana refused to attend the trial. She stayed in her shack, listened to the report of the trial on her radio, and wept, as all Palestine did, when the Irgun boys made patriotic speeches, demanded to be treated as prisoners of war, demanded to be addressed as Hebrew Fighters for Liberation.

But her Joel did not make a speech. He did not wave his fist at the bewigged British judge. And after the verdict, he alone of his comrades did not step disdainfully to the hangman's noose, reciting the psalms of David.

Joel was sentenced to seven years. He served only two years, because by then the British had had it, as the Jewish terrorists had predicted. On May 14, 1948, Sir Alan Cunningham, the last British High Commissioner, sailed from Haifa. Joel was released, with other political prisoners, and he married Miriam. His mother refused to come to the wedding, but she softened a bit when her grandson was born. Joel and Miriam dine at his mother's house every Friday night, and the ordeal is always a kind of penance for Joel and Miriam, and the year is always 1946.

CHAPTER VII

Days of Fire: 1939-1948

✡ "In blood and fire did Judea fall,
    From blood and fire Judea shall rise again."
                    —Anthem of the Irgun, Jewish terrorist
                    organization

There is a notion among historians that the character of a nation, like that of an individual, is molded in its early formative years. The shocks and struggles of emerging, it is held, leave residual traces and emotional scars in the make-up of a country as well as in the make-up of citizens. Thus, anyone who seeks to understand the molded sabra of today, must look carefully at the bitter, grotesque, electric, and often surrealistic events in the Holy Land in the turbulent decade before the whole smoldering mess exploded in 1948 with the declaration of a Jewish state.

The sabra leaders of today, and almost all of Israel's top army officers, came of age in that decade. They helped to shape their young nation's history. They fought the British, they fought the Arabs, and three rival underground groups fought each other. Younger sabras who missed it all have fathers and mothers, older brothers and sisters who endured the days of fire.

The fateful decade was a bloody school for those who cared to learn. There were solicitous teachers and harsh lessons. Hitler taught the sabras that the Jews must have their own scrap of land; Britain taught them how little could be expected from a momentarily benevolent great power (a lesson later taught anew by Charles de Gaulle). The United Nations, having created Israel by international law, and then having stood by impotently in 1948, while five Arab nations tried to wipe out its creature, taught the sabras how helpless were men of good will. The lessons have sunk in deeply.

In the summer of 1942, the future looked very black indeed for the Allied forces who were locked in combat with the awesome German war machine. Russia staggered as German cadres raced toward the Caucasus; British troops fell back across the Libyan desert into Egypt, shattered by Rommel's Afrika Korps. The entire Middle East was threatened by a giant pincer movement. Stalingrad, El Alamein, and the Allied invasion of North Africa were still undreamed of miracles.

For the Jews of Palestine, the situation was doubly grave. Egypt was shaky and contained many openly enthusiastic Nazi supporters; if Egypt fell, Palestine could not be supported. There seemed every likelihood that the Afrika Korps would soon march into Jerusalem and Tel Aviv, and that the Jews of Palestine would inexorably become victims of the fate that had befallen their relatives in Europe: mass extermination.

This, then, was the terrible backdrop—and dilemma—against which a new drama unfolded in the Holy Land: the rise of terrorism against the British even while the Nazi enemy was at the gates. This paradox was at the heart of the deadly struggle between Haganah, Irgun, and the Stern Gang, who often fought each other with more venom than they displayed against the British.

As we have said earlier, with the outbreak of World War II a kind of uneasy truce was reached between the Jewish resistance and the British Mandatory Government. It was a bizarre honeymoon period, but incredibly filled with the violence, mock legality, and bewildering double-dealing that seems to be a specialty of the Middle East. Both Haganah and Irgun leaders were escorted out of British jails and sent on extremely dangerous missions for the Allies, such as parachuting behind enemy lines into the Balkan countries. Altogether thirty-two parachutists from Palestine were sent. The most famous of these was Chana Senesh, a name cherished by every sabra school child; she was a charming young kibbutz girl who was dropped into Hungary, captured by the Gestapo, and after their usual treatment, executed.

In another instance, the Irgun terrorist commander-in-chief, David Raziel, was released from the British detention camp of Latrun, and with a few of his fellow Irgun members flown to Habiniyah, a British airfield near Bagdad. Their mission was to get into Bagdad disguised as Arabs and to blow up the oil installations there. On May 20, 1941, Raziel was killed. The first commander of the terrorist, anti-British Irgun was then buried with full military honors in the British military cemetery in Habiniyah, with the Star of David on his tombstone. This ironic fact is barely known today.

There are dozens of other examples of weird relations between Britain and the Jewish resistance. For example, in 1941 the British needed some particularly tough commandos, familiar with the area, to carry out sabotage in Vichy-held Syria. They approached Haganah, who agreed to supply some good men. A group of boys from the Israeli settlements near the Syrian border went over, blew up bridges, destroyed communication lines, and did an impressive job. One of them was Moshe Dayan, a young sabra from the settlement of Nahalal. Less than a year before, a British military court had sentenced him to a ten-year jail sentence, and Dayan served two years in jail. In the Syrian exploit, four months after his release, Dayan lost one eye and returned home as "an amnestied criminal."

As early as 1939 and 1940, British Police and Army units raided Jewish kibbutzim, which served as Haganah training camps, and arrested all the Haganah leaders they could lay their hands on. Most of the Haganah top brass had already volunteered for action with His Majesty's Forces in the war against Germany; * in one of the astounding events in this curious period, Haganah leaders who were on maneuvers with British units were rounded up at their training camp and tossed in jail. One Haganah man among them was sentenced to life imprisonment; the other forty-two men in the unit were given sentences of ten years' imprisonment. Later, their sentences were halved, and they reappeared in British uniforms on Egyptian battlefields.

These cockeyed, tragi-comic antics between the British authorities and the Haganah lurched on all through World War II. Haganah men were condemned as underground rebels, handed down stiff jail sentences, suddenly released a year or two later to embark upon some hair-raising mission for the Allies, then tossed back into a detention camp for the following year.

A word must be said here regarding the special affinity, the romantic, unique, and fascinating relationship between Britain and the Jews. It was only *after* the generous British commitment of the Balfour Declaration that the "happy chemistry" between them lost its potency.

For nineteenth-century Englishmen, the Bible had been adopted, in Thomas Huxley's phrase, as "the national epic

---

* The war effort of Haganah, to say nothing of the thirty thousand Palestinaian Jews in British uniform, was the best kept secret of the war in the Middle East.

of Britain." The Old Testament and its prophecies were the very core of British fundamentalism, and the English embraced the stern God of Abraham as their very own. They were also repeatedly outspoken about the Christian debt of conscience to the people of the Book. Emotionally, the British always had, so to say, one foot in Palestine. As a direct outgrowth of all this sentiment, carried along on the currents of British imperial ambition, came the impetus for a Jewish Palestine. As Barbara Tuchman has remarked, "It is a curious irony that the Jews retrieved their home partly through the operation of the religion they gave the gentiles."

As early as August 17, 1840, an editorial had appeared in the *London Times,* urging a plan "to plant the Jewish people in the land of their fathers." This fantastic notion was advanced by Lord Ashley (later Lord Shaftesbury). The planting was to be "secured under the protection of a European power"—Britain. Lord Palmerston was also in favor of Jewish settlement in the Holy Land, as an outpost for the British Empire. George Eliot's flaming story of 1876, *Daniel Deronda,* remains the best Zionist tract ever written by a Gentile.

Land of Gilead, a book by a flamboyant, religious eccentric, the Englishman Lawrence Oliphant, inspired Russian-Jewish students with the idea of returning to the desolate and impoverished Holy Land. Oliphant actually went to Palestine to survey the country and made several trips to Constantinople to persuade the Turkish Sultan to grant to the Jews a charter of colonization, a million-and-a-half acre colony for settlement east of the Jordan, connected by rail to Haifa, and thence to the Suez Canal itself. Forgetting, as Gentiles often did, that Jews who wanted to go to Palestine were not Rothschilds, but rather were dead broke, Oliphant painted for the Sultan a glowing picture of the advantages of securing as an ally this "wealthy, powerful, and cosmopolitan race." The scheme collapsed, but Oliphant later settled in Haifa and died there.

Arthur Balfour, the pro-Zionist British Foreign Minister in the Lloyd George Cabinet of 1917, the man responsible for the Declaration which bears his name, received his boyhood training in the Old Testament from his mother. In 1925, Lord Wedgewood proposed the idea of a Jewish state as the seventh dominion in the British Commonwealth. In sum, if there ever was a Christian people who benevolently loved the Jews, it was the British. There even was a "British Israel" group who were persuaded that the Anglo-Saxons stem from the Ten Lost Tribes of Israel. Indeed, England's green and pleasant land often seemed, in the rosy glow of victorianism, the New Jerusalem. An Englishman, surveying with self-satisfaction the far-flung ramparts of his Empire, valiantly shouldering the white man's burden, could also feel with some emotion that he too was ordained and Chosen.

These admirable, rather touching British conceits should be kept in mind while reading the rather harsh documentation in this chapter of how Christian love (marching hand in hand with aims of Empire) transmogrified into tragic enmity with the very Jews whom the British had welcomed back to the Land. It is one of the more tragic twists of history in our time.

For almost immediately after World War II the tolerant, decent British had become the most anti-Semitic people in Europe. By 1946, British soldiers heiled Hitler in Jewish kibbutzim, British Police mirthfully painted swastikas on Jerusalem synagogues, Jewish shop windows were smashed in Liverpool and Glasgow, and a cheering crowd of thousands stood on the docks of Liverpool to receive as a hero Roy Farran, an ex-officer of the Palestinian Police, who had been recently acquitted of the charge of killing a sixteen-year-old Jewish boy of Jerusalem.

When the first Jewish settlements were founded in Palestine in the 1870's, the land was under Turkish rule. Jews were forbidden to possess arms. There was at that time nothing remotely resembling public law and order. An infidel non-Moslem who wandered about Palestine could be casually murdered for his boots, let alone for his donkey. The Jewish colonists survived by one means alone: by firing back against Arab raiders, by proving to their Arab neighbors that the Jews were ready to defend themselves, and were not cowards and "sons of death," as the Arab phrase has it.

This led to the rise of the *Shomrim,* a kind of Wild West rangers who guarded the Hebrew farms, and to the formation of the famous Jewish self-defense militia, the Haganah.

When the British succeeded the Turks as rulers of Palestine, after World War I, Jews were still forbidden to bear arms, except for a few antiquated shotguns. The boys and girls of Haganah, therefore, buried their arms in unlikely places around their kibbutzim when the British inspectors appeared, and took them out when the Arabs attacked.

Haganah means defense, and the proud slogan of the Haganah was *Havgalah,* self-restraint. It shunned the policy of civil warfare and vendettas against the Arabs, and bloody opposition to the British. As there were roughly two Arabs to one Jew in Palestine in 1939, and the British policy toward the Jews had swung to an openly pro-Arab stand, self-restraint was no easy matter.

The striking arm of Haganah was called the "Palmach," and was made up of tough youngsters. (In the War of Liberation in 1948, the Palmach was led by the sabra Yigal Allon, who at the present writing is Israel's Deputy Prime Minister.) Many of them had been trained by the remarkable British Captain Orde Wingate, later General Wingate of Burma fame in World War II. He had arrived in Palestine in 1931 on a routine posting. Wingate was a burning Christian Zionist of the mystic brand, and at once began recruiting members of Haganah for his maquis-type "Special Night Squads." They called him the "Lawrence of the Jews." The young *Palmachniks* (including Moshe Dayan and Moshe Carmel, the latter today Israel's Minister of Transportation) adored this dynamic British Officer who was inspired by an emotional identification with the Jews and the dream of Zion restored. On the eve of Wingate's enforced departure from Palestine, he tried passionately to convince the Haganah leaders that the Jews, if they were to achieve a Jewish state, would have to fight Britain to get it.

Service in the Palmach, before it was disbanded and replaced by the Israeli Army, was a proud honor that attracted girls as well as boys. (One of those girls was the coauthor of this book.)

From World War II onward, the position of the moderate Haganah, caught between the British authorities and those two apostles of violence, the Irgun and the Stern Gang, was agonizing. The British accused all three Jewish groups of diabolical deeds. More grave, the authorities used the violent acts of the two small terrorist groups as an excuse to crush the far more powerful and peaceable Haganah, which had the militant support of the vast majority of Jews within Palestine.

In 1944, both the Irgun and the Stern Gang stepped up their anti-British terrorism. Irgun blew up several government buildings, and even occupied, temporarily, the British Broadcasting Service at Ramallah. The Stern Gang nearly assassinated Sir Harold MacMichael, the man whom many Jews held personally responsible for the *Struma* disaster. The Sternists, as mentioned before, also got two men into Cairo and managed to kill Lord Moyne, Britain's Resident Minister in the Middle East.

The assassination of Lord Moyne by Jewish fanatics set off

a shudder of revulsion throughout the world. Responsible Jewish leaders in Palestine new that if such violence went on unabated, world opinion, until now largely sympathetic, would turn away in horror from the Zionist cause. This had to be averted at any price. The Jewish terrorists, therefore, were now considered by most Jews to be the archenemy. The Jewish Agency, in its role of the responsible Jewish body in Palestine, now recruited Haganah to destroy the Irgun and the Stern Gang.

The explosive nature of this decision, the charged emotion it set off—and which still reverberates in Israel—is difficult to describe. The order meant brother against brother, father against son. After arduous soul-searching, Haganah decided to go through with it, agreed to break up and betray its rivals. The repugnance at being cast into the role of British informers against fellow Jews was strong, but the fear that the Haganah might be crushed, and with it the entire militant Zionist movement, was stronger. Shortly after the murder of Lord Moyne, the British Police received a list of names and secret addresses of four hundred leading Irgun and Stern Gang members. That list was supplied by Haganah.

Jew betrayed Jew. The mere discussion of the shameful act, which is ironically referred to as "the season," still arouses passion today in Israel, with partisans of both sides still fervently convinced of its right or wrong.

Nevertheless, the terrorism went on. One of the clear lessons of our century is that an underground movement that is ruthlessly dedicated to its cause cannot be aborted short of savage destruction in the style of the Germans and the Russians of our time. This Haganah was not prepared to do.

In desperation, Haganah decided that at the very least, they could do a far better job of curbing the terrorists than the British were doing. Haganah, a technically illegal body, proceeded to enforce the King's Peace by kidnapping their underground rivals.

In December 1944 and January 1945, picked Haganah squads hunted down a number of Irgun and Stern Gang members and known sympathizers and carried them off to "politically reliable" kibbutzim, which were also at this time Haganah guardhouses.

The British, rather than viewing Haganah with new affection for this thoughtful aid, intensified its attack on Haganah itself. In one ludicrous case in January 1945, a young Haganah member, the bodyguard of Moshe Sharett (later Prime Minister of Israel), was sentenced to six-months' imprisonment for being caught in the possession of a revolver and fourteen cartridges. The irony here is that Sharett, as the British well knew, was leading the Haganah war against the terrorists.

On May 8, 1945, Germany capitulated to the Allies.

*   *   *

The end of the war, the collapse of fascist Germany, and the victory of the Labor party in Britain raised high the hopes of the Jews of Palestine. The implacable British attitude, it was now confidently believed, would be altered. After all, the new men in Whitehall were socialist brothers and solemnly committed to a pro-Zionist pledge in the Labor platform.

But as so often is the case in history, an altogether undreamed of human element now entered the scene. That subjective factor was the personality and tenacity, the blind, pigheaded, emotive bias of the new Labor Government's Foreign Minister, Mr. Ernest Bevin. Bevin's role in the swaying fate of Palestine is a fascinating example of the ever-present human quirk in affairs of state, "the imponderabilia without which life is not life, history not history, and a people no people."

History could not have tossed up a more improbable figure to deal with the bewildering tangle of Palestine, and the homeless remnants of the Nazi Holocaust, then the burly, pugnacious, ignorant trade-union boss, Mr. Bevin. He was a large man, inclined to be boisterous, and his overbearing rough-and-tumble ways had raised him from the ranks of the trade union to his exalted position as Great Britain's Foreign Minister.

The conscience of the world now shrank from the horror of the extermination camps, which could no longer be concealed; Mr. Bevin said in a famous remark in answer to the clamor of the DP's to be sent to Palestine, "If the Jews with all their sufferings want to get too much at the head of the queue, you have the danger of another anti-semitic reaction through it all." The British Government itself arranged for a joint Anglo-American Committee of Enquiry into the Palestine problem; Mr. Bevin could find no time to talk to any of its members. Mr. Bevin declared that the resettlement of DP's in Palestine would cost the British taxpayer two hundred million pounds; the informed world knew that Zionist funds had always carried the entire burden of Jewish settlement in Palestine, and the British taxpayer had never paid a farthing.

He denied that the Labor party had ever passed a resolution endorsing a Jewish state, and added unblushingly, "if ever it was done, it was done in the enthusiasm of a Labor Party Conference." In 1946, in a spectacular breach of international law, he announced the "independent kingdom" of Transjordan, which was part of the territory mandated to Britain's care by the League of Nations.

Bevin was advised by British general J. C. D'Arcy, a veteran of long Middle East service, that "Haganah could hold

Palestine against the entire Arab world"; Mr. Bevin refused
to believe it. When American public opinion swelled up for
the admission of one hundred thousand refugees into Palestine (as recommended by the Anglo-American Committee),
Mr. Bevin remarked that the reason why the Americans were
so keen on dumping Jews into Palestine was that "they did
not want to have too many of them in New York."

Ernest Bevin was a courageous man. He believed, in all
sincerity, that his unyielding stand was best for England.
Constitutional law, solemn mandates, Leagues of Nations
and United Nations were all very well, but Bevin knew what
was best for his mates. Besides, the Jews only showed their
gratitude to their kindly British benefactors by opening fire
on British soldiers as soon as they somehow sneaked into
Palestine.

More Jews were murdered in the two years, 1944 until
1946, than in all the four thousand years of Jewish history;
six million had perished, and only one million European
Jews survived the Holocaust. Of these, one hundred thousand
were a "diseased rump," living in Displaced Persons camps.
A month after Germany capitulated, in 1945, the Jewish
Agency petitioned for the allocation of one hundred thousand
immigration permits for Palestine, "in view of the untenable
position of the surviving Jews of Europe." *

In September, President Truman wrote a letter to Britain's
Prime Minister Attlee, urging him to grant the petition. The
letter, according to a State Department spokesman, went
unanswered. World public opinion now focussed on the
plight of the refugees, and the rescue of the hundred thousand was the first order of business. On September 24, Dr.
Weitzman, disclosed that the Jewish Agency had been offered

* Mr. Atlee, the leader of the British Labor Government, suggested at this
time that the Jewish survivors of the concentration camps should remain
and help rebuild Europe.

fifteen hundred permits instead of a hundred thousand, with the added comment by the British Colonial Office that "these were the last certificates available under the White Paper."

With this announcement, something snapped within the hearts of Palestinian Jews who still believed in British decency, peaceful persuasion, and in the efficacy of petitions, plans, and protests. In Tel Aviv, a silent march of fifty thousand demonstrators was led by men and women who were survivors of Auschwitz and Buchenwald; they walked dressed in the striped pajamas that had been the uniform of the concentration camp inmates.

Haganah, the moderate underground militia, now reluctantly became converted to violence—the same violence, of course, which they had denounced so scathingly when used by Irgun and the Stern Gang. The far-reaching importance of this grim metamorphosis cannot be exaggerated. At long last the majority of Palestinian Jews had decided upon force and active uprising to obtain their ends.

Palmach units broke into Athlit detention camp and freed the Jewish inmates there, refugees who had been scheduled by the British for deportation. One British policeman was killed, the first Englishman ever slain by Haganah in the entire bloody history of the British Mandate in Palestine. On October 31, Haganah launched its first large sabotage action. The Haifa refineries were bombed. British police patrol boats in Jaffa were sabotaged. Six persons were killed in these actions.

Furiously aroused by Haganah's new conversion, the British Labor Government decided to crush Jewish resistance and the Zionist adventure once and for all, with plans put before it by Field Marshal Montgomery. On "Black Saturday," June 30, 1946, the British Army arrested and imprisoned a number of Palestinian Jewish leaders, took over the Jewish Agency building in Jerusalem and rounded up three thousand Jews in key positions who were known to be active in Haganah (including Margalit Banai, who was imprisoned in Latrun).

In the meantime, the Stern Gang was not exactly passive. In one raid on railway installations in Haifa, they were met by bitter fire from the British. The Stern Gang left eleven of their band dead, including several girls. Life in the Holy Land became crazier every day; a British court sentenced a schoolboy to flogging for the crime of carrying illegal leaflets.

On January 24, 1947, the British passed a sentence of death on Dov Gruener, a member of Irgun. Gruener refused to appeal for The King's Clemency, and was scheduled to die. In reprisal, his Irgun comrades kidnapped a British judge and a former British Army officer, and held them as hostages for Gruener. The two Englishmen were released; nevertheless, three months later Gruener was hung, with three other terrorists. Two of the condemned men blew themselves to bits in their prison cells, by pressing smuggled grenades against their armpits. All of them refused to participate in their trial, and sat in court reading the Old Testament and chanting psalms.

On May 6, British plainclothsmen, under orders from Major Roy Farran, D.S.O., dragged off the streets of Jerusalem a sixteen-year-old boy suspected of being a member of the Stern Gang. It was widely believed that the boy was murdered; his body was never found. Farran was tried by a British court-martial and acquitted. He sailed home to England a hero, and an English popular newspaper serialized his memoirs. The Stern Gang killed Farran's brother by sending him a bomb through the mail.

In another incident that shook Palestine, Irgun men broke into the Napoleonic-era fortress of Acre, and released over a hundred of their comrades who were imprisoned there. Some of the attackers were captured by the British and hung.

In reprisal, Irgun captured two British soldiers, hung them in an orange grove, with booby traps attached to their swaying bodies. On July 22, 1947, members of the Irgun blew up the King David Hotel in Jerusalem, headquarters of the British Secretariat. Ninety-one British, Jews, and Arabs died in the explosion.

*   *   *

Meanwhile, the little hell-ships kept arriving at the shores of Palestine with their forbidden human cargo, and were immediately surrounded by Royal Navy destroyers and police launches. Young men and women of Haganah risked their own lives swimming out in the dead of night to rescue the immigrants, in the teeth of British coastal patrols. (In 1948, the coauthor of this book, Herbert Russcol, arrived in Palestine on the *Pan York,* a battered American ex-ferry boat built to accommodate six hundred passengers, and which carried on this not uneventful trip five thousand half-crazed illegals, plus a handful of American volunteers for Haganah.)

A Polish girl's account of the arrival on one of these ships was printed in *Time* magazine (May 6, 1946): "At 11 o'clock at night, our ship arrived. We saw a small light blinking from the Palestinian coast. Towboats came to meet us. . . . One by one we climbed down to them. Everything happened very quickly then. In the boats were Palestinians. They shook hands with us and said, 'Shalom, and welcome home!' When we came on shore, there were more boys and girls from Haganah, and they were armed. We walked through the fields for a few miles . . . I saw young men and women all along the road. Our guides told us that these people were all members of Haganah standing guard for us. . . . There was a chain of them all the way to the shelter of a settlement inland. As we passed them, they smiled and called quietly to us, 'Shalom, Shalom.' "

Most of the miserable arrivals were seized by the British and transferred to the detention camps on the island of Cyprus. Then the Palestinian government, in one of its more lunatic moments, decided that Cyprus was too close to Palestine; perhaps the Jews might figure out a way to get them into the Forbidden Land. The British decided to send all future human cargo back to port of origin, which was usually Germany, where the chimneys of the death camps were, figuratively, still smoking.

In July, the *Exodus 1947* arrived in Palestine, carrying 4550 refugees. They were transferred—naked, kicking, and screaming—to three British transport ships. This wretched armada sailed for forty-six days, in scorching heat, across the Mediterranean, around the coast of Spain, through the English Channel and across the North Sea to Hamburg, with the sickened world press covering every step of that historic journey. It was one of the most humiliating exploits ever undertaken by Great Britain. The *Exodus* was the most publicized event of this entire period of Palestinian history. No Jewish spokesman could have aroused world sympathy for the Jewish plight as eloquently as did Ernest Bevin by ordering the *Exodus 1947* back to Germany.

On July 8, the British confirmed death sentences on Jewish terrorists they had seized. On July 11, the Irgun captured as hostages two army sergeants of British Army Intelligence. The British hung the three Jews in Acre Prison; thirty hours later an Irgun communiqué announced the execution by hanging of the two British sergeants.

There were no more executions in the Holy Land.

It was all too much, even for the ineffable Mr. Bevin. In fact, the first hint that the wall was cracking had come early in the year, when on January 31 the British Government decided to evacuate from Palestine all British women and children, and male civilians in nonessential jobs. This was the first indication that the British were no longer able to cope with Jewish resistance. On February 18, 1947, Britain referred the Palestine question to the United Nations.

It has become clear that two Englishmen have done as much as anyone to spur the creation of modern Israel: Lord Balfour, whose generous vision handed the Jews their legal charter and the all-powerful support of Britain, and Ernest Bevin, whose intractable stand aroused the horror of the world, and who, by refusing any compromise whatever, compelled the Jews to battle it out and thus win the test of nationhood.

We have remarked that the blood-soaked history of this decade is strewn with ironies. Perhaps the greatest irony here is the fact that without the obsessive figure of the British Foreign Minister forcing the issue, all-or-nothing, not troubling to mask his anti-Semitism amidst a world reeling with the nauseous stench of the German crematories, it is really doubtful whether there would be a Jewish state today.*

With the scene moving to Lake Success, at that time the home of the United Nations, a new series of improbable events transpired that can only be soberly explained as miracles, as is so often the case in the story of Israel. Again, subjective and irrational forces prevailed in the inscrutable working of history.

The United Nations Palestine Committee began its debates on October 4. Both the United States and the Russian delegates—on the same side of an issue for the first time in the UN shaky history—came out in favor of partition and the creation of a separate entity that would be Jewish Palestine.

The voting was periously close; the renaissance of the Jew-

* In an intriguing footnote to history, Abba Eban has pointed out that if the Arabs and the British had agreed to let the one hundred thousand Jewish refugees into the country, the Jewish state might never have come into being. "The Jewish case would have lost its urgency."

ish nation after two millenia now swayed in the balance with the undecided vote of that crucial party to the Palestine dispute, the delegate of the Philippine Islands.

On the twenty-seventh the Chief Rabbi of Jerusalem instructed all Jews to pray at the Wailing Wall. Immediately following this, and possibly Divine Intercession, the gentleman from Haiti, who the day before had announced that he would vote against, received new instructions, to vote *for* partition. The Chinese delegate received instructions to abstain. The Greek representative, who had until now abstained, received instruction to vote against.

Other delegates cabled and telephoned for instructions to their governments, from Costa Rica to Afghanistan, from Iceland to Peru. During the three days before the vote in the Committee, and the final vote in the Assembly, not less than twelve delegates changed their minds about the rights and wrongs of the issue. "It looked as if the Marx Brothers were playing General Post, in the lobbies of Lake Success, for the stake of the future of Israel," one British correspondent wrote.

On November 29, the historic and utterly miraculous vote came at last. Thirty-three nations were for the partition plan; thirteen were against; there were ten abstentions, including that of Britain.

Israel was reborn.

All through that unforgettable night, that first Jewish victory since Roman days, the streets of Tel Aviv and Jerusalem and Haifa were jammed with exultant Jews, dancing, drinking the free wine that flowed in every café.

The next day, Palestinian Arabs killed seven Jews in an ambush near Tel Aviv. The underground war against the British now passed into a war of Arab against Jew.

The Jewish-Arab war of 1948, or series of compounded miracles that Israelis call the War of Liberation, has no proper place in this book. But to round off our story here: On May 14, 1948, Sir Alan Cunningham, the last British High Commissioner for Palestine, sailed from Haifa. The British deliberately left behind them a chaotic land without a legal government, without police or public services, confident that the Arab superiority of numbers would triumphantly fill this vacuum. "We decamp ignominiously," wrote Leopold Amery, a former colonial secretary, "amidst carnage and confusion." *

On the same date, the Jews of Palestine proclaimed their independence. Five Arab countries launched a Holy War against them. In less than some forty days of "legal" warfare, the Jews fought them all off. In the first of the "No Alternative," "Never Again," *leitmotifs* that were to be heard in three wars, the new Israelis fought with their backs to the wall, in a tiny land whose borders were less than a hundred miles long, as narrow as fifteen miles wide, with no chance of defense in depth, let alone withdrawal, while the Arabs had all the advantages of immense frontiers and convenient coastlines. Haganah, well trained by the fateful decade, became the nucleus of the Israeli citizen army. It had gone a long road from being a modest, orderly home militia of a minority people, and emerged as the most significant military force in the Middle East.

Thus, in what was perhaps the saddest irony of this entire story, the idea of Israel, conceived and nurtured by a supreme gesture of a British Cabinet in 1917, the Balfour Declaration, was born in blood and tears in 1948 with the most intransigent opposition of Britain. As Barbara Tuchman observed, "As in the American colonies, England had laid the foundation of a state and then resisted the logical development of

* Letter to the *London Times,* May 14, 1948.

what she had begun until the original bond frayed out in bitterness and strife."

The British Foreign Minister was implacable to the end. In his first public statement on the Palestine question, Mr. Bevin had made his famous remark, warning the Jews, "not to get to the head of the queue." Now in twilight of his debacle he saw to it that they would stay down at the tail of the queue. Three full years after the concentration camps of Germany had been opened, six months after the end of the British Mandate in Palestine and the rebirth of a Jewish state, there were still twelve thousand Jewish survivors from Hitler behind barbed wire in British detention camps in Cyprus.

The raging, obsessed figure of Mr. Bevin was yet to be heard from. The bull was gored and dying, but still dangerous. Suddenly, on January 7, 1949, without warning or reason, five British fighter planes from the Suez Canal Zone zoomed into Israel territory. To this day no one clearly knows why. They were promptly shot down by the infant Israel Air Force. A storm of violent protest against Bevin's madness was heard anew in the world. It was too much even for the British Cabinet, and quick action followed. The utter failure of the long war on Zionism had to be confessed publicly. On January 10, His Majesty's Government graciously accorded formal recognition to the State of Israel. Ernest Bevin died the next year.

*   *   *

We have dwelt at length upon the violent events of this gestative decade because we believe that in this long night of drama, the character of the sabras of Israel was shaped and molded.

The bitter failure of democratic means to achieve independence; the indifference of the world to the plight of homeless Jewish refugees (until the spotlighted *Exodus* case was too harsh even for the world's gaze); the ever-present factor of irrational bias against the Jews, the bias that led Mr. Bevin to tell a colleague, with much emotion, "My dear boy, it's either them [the Jews] or us"; British insistence on "unconditional surrender" of the Zionist idea: these were the wounds and blows which resulted in a lasting traumatism that responded with action and force.

The decade was a bloody trial, the kind that determines whether a people will become a nation or die. A new national consciousness and unity of purpose emerged from the bitter struggle. Professor Talmon has noted that "the State of Israel came into being as the result of an armed uprising, an international agreement, and a victorious war. When we look closely, we discover here the very pattern followed by many national movements in history. Except during the postwar period in black Africa, no new nation has ever been formed nor has any old enslaved people ever won independence without undergoing an ordeal of fire—in the first phase, rebellion, in the last, war. It would seem that only through struggle, suffering, and violence is a people held to have proved that it deserves to be recognized as a nation." *

The sabra's supreme trait, as we have stressed repeatedly, is reliance upon his own action, and the resolve to be master of his fate. This was well learned in the decade of "struggle, suffering, and violence."

"Of course only a minority [of the Jews] became terrorists," Talmon adds, "but the vast majority no longer had the heart or the conviction to oppose them." We may go much farther. The children of the vast majority, today's sabras, have learned the clear lesson of the efficacy of force in this sorry world. Ironically, the sons and daughters of Haganah veterans have almost matter-of-factly embraced as a national philosophy the

* J. C. Talmon, Cohen Memorial Lecture, CCNY, 1968.

violence and reprisal that their parents so abhorred when practiced by the Irgun.

This transformation from the profoundly Jewish passivity to fate is vividly shown in the transformation of Haganah itself during this fateful decade. Haganah moved in transition step by step like a character in a well-made play. It began as law-abiding home militia and ended with a grim policy of sabotage and resistance (but not terror) nearly as ruthless as that of its despised rivals.

It is idle to argue whether Haganah or the terrorists decided the final outcome of the British evacuation (still a most lively topic in Israel). History only shrugs, the passionate differences fade, and we see but the consequences. It seems clear, however, that all resistance movements breed partisans who range from cautious moderates to reckless extremists. It also appears that the extremists are always vilified at first, until the unconscionable rush of events makes them seem like patriotic visionaries.

As a result of Israel's "Days of Fire," there emerged a new kind of Jew. He had none of the Jewish neurosis; he is a kind of Jew the world has not seen since the Jewish-Roman wars.

This Jew is the sabra. His forceful nature, abruptness, his rather rude articulation of speech, his directness, his impatience with endless talk and hypocrisy are but indications of the spartan values he cherishes most: a taut coolness, a self-confident pride, a tight-lipped guarding of sentimental "Jewish" emotion; an insistent demand for thinking and doing which are *tachliss* (Yiddish for practical reality); a contempt for the soft neurasthenic Jew of other lands; and above all bravery and a tough readiness to act and to die on his feet. All the sabra leaders in the political arena today have these *realpolitik* qualities to their fingertips.

Britain has loomed large in these pages. The State of Israel and our sabras exist because of the British and in spite of the British. It is not inapt, therefore, that we close this study of the shaping of the sabra with some recent words of Mr. Harold Macmillan, the former British Prime Minister, and thus himself a successor to the Labor Cabinet of Attlee and Bevin. For the student of Israel's modern history, Mr. Macmillan's remarks, made some months after the Six Days' War, are deliciously (and unintentionally) ironic. They should be savored slowly.

At a New York luncheon in his honor in January 1968, Harold Macmillan was asked what sort of future he envisaged for Britain. Devoid of empire, did it lie along the lines of another Sweden or another Athens, as some had suggested? Macmillan pondered a while, then said:

Not another Athens. The people who suggest that have not read their history. Athens was based on slave labor, ran a powerful empire, fought great wars, and eventually decayed and died. It may well be that Britain will someday follow in the footsteps of Sweden, but if so I'm glad I won't be here to see it.

No, the future I hope for Britain is more like that of Israel. In the time of Elizabeth we were only two million people, in the time of Marlborough only five or six million, in the time of Napoleon only ten million. The other day, while the world debated, Israel's three millions imposed their will on their enemies. They had what any great people need—resolution, courage, determination, pride. These are what really count in men and nations.*

* As quoted in *Saturday Review,* New York, January 27, 1968.

Part Two ✡ THE SABRAS

COME OF AGE

CHAPTER VIII

The Big Change

✡ "I simply do not understand our youth."
> —Secretary of Mapai, Israel's largest Labor party, in 1951

"The old socialist ideals have nothing whatever to do with the kind of people who nowadays live in Israel."
> —Moshe Dayan, speech to Mapai Labor Congress, 1963

For a full twenty years in Israel—until the Six Days' War—hardly a curtain went up on a new Hebrew play without revealing a surly, monosyllabic sabra sprawled on a chair. He was a rather gloomy young man who appeared to be suffering. We were soon told that he spent all his spare time sitting in expresso cafés and dancing the *tvist* in cellar discotheques.

In the second act, there was always a weather-beaten old-timer who raised his hands toward the balcony and asked: What's wrong with young people today? Why have they deserted the ideals of pioneering? After the heroic example of their parents, who wrested a state, who made the desert bloom, why is the sabra longing for the fleshpots of Tel Aviv?

Putting it more bluntly some years back, Avraham Shapira, the last of the legendary turn-of-the-century "Bilu" settlers, addressed a meeting of young people in Tel Aviv and shouted, "You're youth, are you? You're——." This speech caused a furore, and has entered into the popular literature, along with pithy sayings of Theodor Herzl. "You're youth, are you?" sabras would say to one another, mockingly, and with some despair.

The despair was accompanied by some interesting symptoms of guilt and split personality, and brought about, by and large, a troubled and unhappy generation. The trouble was that the glamor had gone out of pioneering and the fires of idealism had been banked. The sons of the pioneers were skeptical about the rewards of the spirit that pioneering offered. They were not stirred by the prospect of eating meals of carrots and potatoes, and then excitedly dancing the hora, while the great majority of the citizenry were doing very well in the cities.*

They winced when they heard the old flaming slogans of Zionism: The Redemption of the Desert, The Religion of Work, and all the other clarion calls that had swept up an earlier generation. As far as the sabra could make out, the original premise of Zionism was bankrupt. This premise, it is often forgotten, held that Jews should live in Zion. It was naïvely believed that with the creation of a Jewish state, Jews from all over the world would immediately and joyfully arrive to help build it. But only a comparative handful of Jews came, unless they were fleeing real or threatened persecution. And nothing shook the hopeful Israelis more in the 1950's than what happened in Algeria. There, the substantial

* Professor Joseph Ben David of the Hebrew University in Jerusalem has put the problem in sociologese: "With the second generation reaching adulthood . . . the problem of moral discontinuity between the collectivistic value of the pioneering period on the one hand, and the complex present-day situation on the other, is perceived as increasingly acute." (*Conforming and Deviant Images of Youth in a New Society*—Ben David, Transactions of the Fifth World Congress of Sociology.)

Jewish population, uprooted by anti-Semitism and political events after living more than two millenia in that land, much preferred settling in France rather than joining their brethren in Israel.

The sabra was also profoundly cynical of Jews abroad who called themselves Zionists, and yet who hung on to affluent America or South Africa or Argentina, rather than going up to Zion now that there was such a place on the map. So derisive had the sabra become that even today among young sabras the word Zionism, in Hebrew, is a slang expression of contempt. It means baloney. "Don't give me any of that *Zionut*," a teen-ager will say to his pal, and it is a good thing the visiting Hadassah ladies cannot understand his Hebrew.

The older pioneer generation beheld their youngsters with dismay. From 1948 until the war of 1967 politicians of every shade, educators, and newspaper editorials regularly denounced the sabras with Old Testament wrath. They were scathingly called the Expresso Generation, the Golden Youth, and accused of dancing before the Golden Calf of radio transistors and washing machines and motorcycles.

Nothing helped. The breach widened between fathers and sons. The kibbutzim shrank from 12 to less than 3 per cent of the population, and were hard-pressed to refill their dwindling ranks. The sabra shrugged sardonically, lounged at midnight at his beloved outdoor cafés in Tel Aviv and Haifa and Jerusalem, sipped his expresso, leafed through his sex-cum-*politika* magazines and watched the girls go by in their miniskirts.

This, in brief, was the Big Change, the crisis in values that wracked Israel for a generation until the Six Days' War. We had been a heady mixture of self-sacrificing idealists; we had become, by and large, "just like everyone else"—materialistic and reluctant idealists. If there was one subject that bored the sabra, it was nostalgic stories about "the good old days."

As any old timer will tell you with a sigh, life before 1948 was wonderful in Palestine, make no mistake about that. Even if you lived in town, rather than on a farm, your values were lofty. There was something shameful in being *lo productivi*—a merchant or middleman, as Jews usually had been in Europe. (Even today a sabra would rather be anything but a shopkeeper.) Building up the country meant you were a teacher or a poet or a stevedore at the new Tel Aviv port.

Arthur Koestler has caught this romantic period, reminiscing from his own experience in Palestine,

Tel Aviv, the first Hebrew city, was a pioneer city dominated by young workers of both sexes in their teens and twenties. The streets belonged to them; khaki shirts, shorts, and dark sunglasses were the fashionable wear, and ties, nicknamed "herrings," a rarity. In the evening, when the cool breeze from the sea relieved the white glare of the day, they walked arm in arm over the hot asphalt of the new avenues through whose chinks the yellow sand oozed up and which ended abruptly in the dunes. At night they built bonfires and danced the hora on the beach, and at least once a week they dragged pompous Mayor Dizengoff or old Rabbi Hertz out of their beds and took them down to the sea to dance with them. They were hard-working, sentimental and gay. They were carried by a wave of enthusiasm which had a crest and no trough . . . the cheap cafés sold meals on credit and got their supplies on credit; landlords let rooms on credit in their houses which were built on credit; and yet the town, instead of collapsing into the sand on which it was built, waxed and grew. . . . Ah, those were the good old times, the legendary days! *

Even in the late 1940's money did not matter much. You did not judge people by their clothes, or by how many rooms they had. On the contrary, when Herbert Russcol searched for a living room, bedroom, and kitchen in Tel Aviv (and

* Arthur Koestler. *Thieves in the Night.* Macmillan, 1946.

paid $2,000 key money to get it), people stared at him in amazement. Why on earth did a single man need a whole flat with three rooms and a private kitchen and bathroom? Whole families then were often crowded into a single room. Why couldn't he rent a spare room in someone's apartment, as most single people did? "You spoiled Americans," he was brusquely told time and again. "We have more important things to think about."

It really didn't matter. These were pulse-quickening days, a time of ecstasy. You felt intensely alive; it was Year One of the Jewish Rebirth, and you were in the middle of it all.

And then, incredibly, came the millenium and the Jewish state. The beautiful myth turned into changed reality, and anticlimax and disillusion were inevitable. We had lived for years with the fond belief that once the golden age would be ushered in, all problems would solve themselves automatically; and then they did not. You could feel the sudden evaporation of idealism in the very air, as this country of underground rebels all at once remembered that they were private people and began worrying about education and good jobs and flats and futures.

It was all perfectly understandable. No one can live in a permanent state of revolution, and all heroes and heroics end by being bores. No longer were Israelis content to dress in khaki shorts and open white shirts. A kibbutz woman no longer took pride in the fact that she owned but one cotton dress. No longer were mixers, refrigerators, phonographs, cars, and all the rest despised luxuries. The chasm between the haves and the have-nots now loomed very large. Before the Big Change, that chasm was not visible—and visibility makes all the difference. For example, two comrades had fought side by side for years in Haganah and neither knew nor cared what the other did in his "daytime job"; then comes the revolution, and one is a high government officer and the other a lowly shoe salesman. "How glorious was communism under the Czar!" was the bitter quip one heard now on the bus to work. "The wonderful dream has come true, and nothing has taken its place."

The joys of statehood brought in its wake another development that was, ironically, a blow to the old ideals: mass immigration. Between 1948 and 1967 over a million immigrants streamed to our shores, people who were not pioneers but refugees who were contemptuous of the brave experiments of the kibbutzim of Galilee, and who wanted to live more or less as they had been living in the shuks of Tangiers or in the suburbs of Bucharest. They wanted to open a kiosk in Jaffa or a dress shop in Jerusalem; they knew nothing of the holy tenets of kibbutz life and cared less. The new immigrants regarded Israel's kibbutz farmers as a bit off, misfits who couldn't make a go of city living; they read about government subsidies to the hard-pressed kibbutzim and scoffed at them as pensioners of the state.

You could see the Big Change in the face of the kibbutznik when he entered Tel Aviv in the 1950's and the 1960's, the disillusion and the bitterness. Before, when a kibbutznik on his vacation strolled down the streets of Tel Aviv, he was greeted deferentially; he was the elite of the nation, and his faded khaki and open sandals were honored badges. He was was a prince with a begging bowl. He belonged to Israel's chosen few, those who had elected to forsake all, yea, and go into the desert.

Life, in a way, has passed him by. (Although idealism has returned since the Six Days' War.) The kibbutz was absolutely necessary a generation ago, but today it is an anachronism. As J. L. Talmon has put it, "the philosophy which glorified the university graduate who exchanged his pen or scalpel for a spade or a hammer became irrelevant when the country was suddenly swamped with hundreds of thousands of newcomers who could handle nothing else but a spade."

The kibbutznik sees that has friends who stayed in the cities have homes, and a future, and were vacationing in Turkey last summer. He does not come to Tel Aviv anymore unless he cannot help it.

*   *   *

In a fascinating way, what happened in Israel appears to be strikingly similar to the "Revolt of the Grandchildren" which is going on today in Soviet Russia. For our own tired slogans, "The Ingathering of the Exiles," "The Redemption of the Desert," read "The Dictatorship of the Proletariat" and "Heroic Soviet Youth On Guard for Peace," and you have much the same story.

Like the Russian young women of today, whose mothers proudly dug the Moscow subways and found it exhilarating to labor side by side with men in heavy industry, our sabra girls are no longer stirred by such prospects. Like the new Russians, our sabras are acquisitive in what is rapidly becoming a would-be middle-class society. That little house, that little car, that long-dreamed-of vacation on the Greek islands are the goals that most young people in the West work toward.

It is not surprising, therefore, that the man to read on the Big Change in Israel is the Yugoslav Communist Milovan Djilas. His famous treatise, "The New Class," seems to apply with remarkable accuracy to all revolutionary societies from Moscow to Ghana. These new societies were born out of revolutions that had a common dream: freedom from an oppressor, social justice, and the yearning to express a national culture. The personal life and ambitions of the rebels are subject to the collective interest. With victory, Djilas observes, there is a gap, a sense of anticlimax; the goal of revolution has been achieved and no new rallying cry unites the country.

With victory, life is far worse for many of the victors. Before, "they," the hated despots, held power and all the top jobs; status differences between the insurgents seem temporary and unimportant—after the revolution all that will be changed. The success of the great cause does indeed bring about social changes, but not those that had been expected. Instead of fraternity and equality, there emerge new social inequalities. Some ex-underground heroes get supreme power; others wind up as drudges at the post office. This causes new tensions and bitterness.

The older generation righteously condemns its "decadent" children and points virtuously to its own heroic past; the children shrug, and dress like the Beatles, or lounge about in expresso cafés.

"The heroic era . . . is past. The epoch of its great leaders has ended [read: Ben-Gurion]. The epoch of practical men has set in [read: Eshkol and Golda Meir]. The new class has been created. It is at the height of its power and wealth, but it is without new ideas. It has nothing more to tell the people. The only thing that remains is for it to justify itself." *

*   *   *

For the sabra, what is most ironic about the whole business is that while he is pilloried for turning to a *decadenti* way of life, it was his father who first began worshipping before the Golden Calf. It was the young people of a generation ago, the immigrant pioneers themselves, who rushed toward normalcy with an apprehensive concern to "make something" of themselves, now that the battle for a state had been won.

The hypocrisy of this has not escaped the sabra and has intensified his contempt for *Zionut*, empty phrases. He knows that the same parent who today pays lip service to the old beliefs by encouraging his boy or girl to put on a blue shirt on Friday nights and join other youngsters in the Youth

* Djilas, *The New Class*, Prager, New York, 1957

Movement in singing "We Shall Build the Galilee!" would usually be aghast if the same youngster took the notion seriously and struck out for a kibbutz. Most parents today want their children to be professional men and women. That, too, is the Big Change.

But this troubled era came to an abrupt end with the Six Days' War. The spirit in the air is again much as it was in the good old days. Zionism is fashionable once more, but there is a new conception of Zionism, being a fierce patriotism, rather than a mystique that demanded you live a monastic life on the land. You do not have to dig potatoes and ride on a tractor—*just be here.* Don't worry, there will be plenty of sacrifices for you to make, with the Russians on our doorstep, as well as the sea of Arabs.

Nobody sneers at the Expresso Generation anymore. The sabra, with his extraordinary bravery, saved the country from annihilation. The much-abused sabra, of all people, returned Jerusalem. By doing so he has paid his bill—to himself, to his parents, to the six million dead.

He does not have to envy his father and mother, tell himself they were lucky, they lived in heroic days. He is not sheepish any longer because he is not up on a godforsaken kibbutz, the way they were. He does not have to avert his eyes as he passes the family portraits in the living room—browning snapshots of his parents in their tent on a Spartan farm, with a touching look about them of fervor and asceticism and moral earnestness. He can be complacent, as his father reminisces about the time his Haganah unit launched an attack on a British police fortress in 1947, or as his mother repeats the stories of how she swam out up to her neck to drag in to shore the illegal immigrants from the forbidden ships. He has his own stories to tell his children now.

It is a great country, come on over and break your head. But first, pull up a chair and have an expresso.

C H A P T E R   I X

Love, Israeli Style

✡ "Thou art beautiful, O my love, comely as Jerusalem,
   terrible as an army with banners."

                                        —Song of Songs

Many Israeli banknotes are engraved with a picture of an appealing, full-breasted girl soldier. She is standing before a strip of farmland, which she guards with her life. She is fearless, winsome, and a few pounds overweight. Because she carries a gun and shoots it well, she possesses a glamor all her own, unlike that of women in other lands. This girl is the national image of the sabra.

She has captured the imagination of the world. There has even been a Hollywood film about Israel in which the fiery heroine was called by the impossible name of "Sabra." She is natural and unaffected and there is a pioneer freshness about her. She is contemptuous of doll-like women who paint their faces, and whose lives revolve around the pleasures of shops and dressmakers. She has more important things to think about. She is a serious and idealistic human being.

And yet, we have heard, she enjoys earthy love-making on the red clay of the Negev or under the stars of Galilee, and does not give a damn what anyone thinks. If she wants a man she is direct and disarmingly frank about it, entirely without wiles. She is her own woman, unafraid of love or Arab bullets. She is the modern goddess Diana of the Hunt, and her bow is the Uzi submachine gun, Israel army issue.

We in Israel are very proud of her. She is our leading tourist attraction, even more than Jerusalem's Wall. Everybody wants to see the sabra girls. Jewish women have always had a reputation for beauty, and Israel's sun and diet have worked new wonders—they are lovelier than ever. The young Israeli girls are as lissome as the Italians, as brave as the *partizana* women of Yugoslavia, and—godsend to travelers—they speak English.

Since the birth of the state in 1948, we have had Jews from more than a hundred lands streaming to our shores, often intermarrying, and the sabras now come in bewildering varieties. There are grave, black-eyed, slim-boned girls from Yemen, whose dusky beauty can make a usually reasonable man howl at the moon. There are seventh-generation sabras who are blonde, Aryan-looking, and possess the strapping figures of the girls of Sweden.

All this can be heady wine for the eager male traveler to Israel. He remembers that we are Mediterranean—the scorching sun produces women as sultry as the Spanish and the Italians (no one remembers that the same sun beats upon the unusually beautifully women of Greece). We are Levantine—he has a vision of flashing eyes in forbidden courtyards, and delights of love unknown to graduates of Vassar College. And, never-to-be-forgotten allure—the sabra girl carries a gun. It is a simple matter to meet her; so much of life in Israel is crowd life, in bus queues, in outdoor cafés, on the beaches. The traveler is urged by his acquaintances in Israel to leave the guided tours, rent a car, get on the road, and explore the real Israel by himself. He readily complies.

Unless he comes between November and April, there is almost never a drop of rain, and our visitor hires an open car and heads for the countryside. The entire youth of the nation, especially on weekends, seem to be on the move to somewhere. They are riding in jeeps, on Italian motorcycles, and hordes of them pass, standing up on the backs of rickety trucks. Hitchhiking appears to be the national pastime, and our visitor beholds at every turn young students, kibbutzniks, other tourists, and boys and girls in uniform. There is a gay camaraderie in the air, an innocent brashness as the truckloads pass him by, and sabras wave at him as they lustily sing Hebrew songs. The visual separations of wealth—expensive clothes, impressive cars—are absent. If the visitor has rented a flashy American car he feels sheepish about it now.

He is happy. He feels healthy. If he is no longer young, he feels young at the sight of all those shouting youngsters about him. If he is American, he has put on his quietest sport shirt so that no one will guess that he is American. At every traffic light there are pretty girls in uniform waiting for a *tramp,* as a hitchhike is called in sabra slang, and our traveler, who probably would never have dreamed of picking up a stranger back home, jams on his brakes before the prettiest. She hops in. It is that simple.

She glances at him and thanks him in lilting English. She takes off her army cap, tosses her hair about her shoulders, and settles down contentedly. The traveler feels marvelous. The sun is beating fiercely and it is all rather like an Italian film.

He strikes up a conversation and they chat. She seems interested in him and asks intelligent questions about his life back home. She asks him how it is possible, now that we have a Jewish state, that all the Jews do not move here immediately. He finds himself explaining with some eloquence the virtues of life in the good old U.S.A. She listens intelligently. After a while they are speaking with the naturalness of friends. The sabra speaks simply and directly to the point, he notes with approval, and there is no false coquetry about her. They are two mature human beings, and there is none of the predictable ploys of the chance encounters with women that he had known in the past.

The landscape is wonderful; the fields are ablaze with poppies and sunflowers, and a lacework of terraces embroider the small hills. He finds it all moving in a way which he cannot explain. He glances at his companion beside him, and she seems like a rose of Sharon herself. He politely remarks that the girls of Israel all seem to have smashing figures, and she laughs and tells him it is because they spend so much time at the beach—a sabra girl would rather die than appear ungainly in a bikini. She tells him amusing stories, such as that even the sabra girls whose parents came from Morocco or Algiers are fanatical weight watchers now, although in the lands where they came from a man paid far more dowry for a nice fat wife than for a scrawny one.

After an hour he pauses before a roadside café and invites her to join him in a soft drink, perhaps a sandwich. She accepts without comment, and he hastens to open the door of the car for her. She laughs and tells him that a sabra boy would never do that. What is she, an invalid? The café is jammed with young people, mostly dressed in khaki, and there is a sense of exhilaration and excitement in the air. He searches for a chair for her, and she protests and fetches her own. What is she, a *matronita?* She tells him, with good humor, that she is not one of the pampered dolls he is accustomed to. The sabra girls are equal to men in every way, and have overcome all these trappings of a *decadenti* bourgeois culture.

They sip their drinks and cool off. She smiles at him and seems to enjoy his company. He feels that with a girl like this it is the man's innate qualities that would attract her—

not his bankbook, nor his social status—the *man*. Diffidently he tells her how wonderful it is to speak to a girl as one human being to another, without the shabby bag of flirtatiousness that always went with it. She smiles. He asks her if she is in a hurry to get home. She replies that she is in no hurry, she is perfectly free. He gulps, takes a deep breath, and asks her if she would do him the honor of spending a few hours with him and show a bit of the country to a lonely visitor.

She claps her hands with enthusiasm and thinks it an excellent idea. She loves sports cars, she says, and she hasn't been on a jaunt for ages. Where shall it be, South to the Negev? North to Galilee? To *Galil*. She will show him the loveliest part of Israel. Carried away with her natural response, the lack of the worldly-wise glance that his request would have elicited in a *decadenti* woman of another country, he puts his hand on hers, impulsively. She squeezes his hand in return, firmly.

The landscape takes on a mystic quality and the approaching hills of Galilee are round as a woman's body. Our couple talk animatedly now, about everything under the sun. Our visitor feels lighthearted and carefree. He asks her questions about sabras, and she explains their outlook on life. How they are proud to earn their own living, never to be dependent upon a man. How can a self-respecting woman put up with a subservient role? She explains that a sabra seeks a comrade in a man, neither a provider nor a status symbol. She tells him of the fierce fight of the women of Palestine forty years ago for the right to work alongside of the men in the fields, and the right to make love if they desired to. The famous sabra bravery didn't just appear now, she reminds him gravely; twenty years ago, in the underground army of Palmach, in the days when they fought the British, the girls insisted on taking part along with the boys in the strenuous exercise called "omega," even though warned that it was injurious to the womb.

It is afternoon when they reach Lake Tiberias, and she proposes a swim. He says regretfully that he has no bathing suit. Neither have I, she laughs, forget your bourgeois notions. We are mature people, and besides, we're friends now, aren't we? He shakily agrees, and sternly tells himself to cast off his traces of *decadenti* culture. She runs like a deer toward the water, undresses unconcernedly, and he has an aching glimpse of sweet bosom and firm torso.

They ride on, after their swim, refreshed and gay. They pass all sorts of crumbling stones and she explains to him to which period of Palestinian history they belong. Twilight falls, and our visitor notes that his charming companion makes no mention of leaving his side. He has a subliminal memory of Ingrid Bergman and a sleeping bag. They ride in silence in the gentle darkness and reach one of the resthouses for travelers that the kibbutzim maintain in the area in wooded, romantic settings.

Without further comment, the sabra girl tells him that this would be a lovely place for them to spend the night. He nods wordlessly, not quite sure that all this is happening to him. In the modest lounge the receptionist does not seem at all surprised that they have arrived without luggage and asks if they want one room or two? Of course only one, the sabra says without hesitation; it's a pity for the money.

Moments later they are in a secluded cabin and very much alone. They gaze outside where the soft hills are quiet in their archaic slumber. The stars are brilliant and heaven is close. The traveler turns to this beguiling creature and with unbearable yearning takes her into his arms. And then, pow!

The rude awakening. The wish-fantasy is over. She advises him furiously that she hasn't the slightest intention of making love with him just because he invited her on a jaunt and bought her a sandwich. She is not one of his bourgeoise dolls that he can buy this way. Our shattered visitor either lies and protests that this was the last thing he had in mind, or else his voice takes on a nasty tinge as he accuses her of leading him on; and what about the single room she booked for the two of them? "Well, what about it?" she replies with indignation, she was only saving him money.

Slow curtain against rising voices.

Now in this little comedy of manners our sabra has been perfectly honest, according to her code. She liked him, she really wanted to go on a trip, and her conduct was innocent. There was no built-in promise on her part. How could he think otherwise? The sabras are above that. If he is used to such *degenerati* behavior back where he came from, well, she can't help that.

It is merely a communication gap, as the Americans solemnly say. It is a basic sabra trait of ingenuousness. They are forthright and without guile. Their social skin has not yet taken on the layers of polite hypocrisies that most of us have acquired. Whether the foreigner realizes it or not, it is he who has from childhood learned the insinuations, the little fictions that make life more manageable.

The sabras are proud of being *yashar l'inyan,* direct to the point, impatient of frills and artifice, and intensely unaffected. In our story, for example, the girl might have asked him without hesitation how much money he earned. This is informational and interesting. A girl from another culture would never ask, but would perhaps sketch their man-woman relationship according to his hints as to his income.

Tourism is very important to Israel's economy, and we hasten to assure the perhaps dismayed reader that our little vignette does not always end in this abrupt fashion. She may decide, our sabra, that it is to be a romance, but it is her decision.

To understand her we must remember that she is by determination as different as possible from her grandmother, who lived a walled-in, religious, tradition-ridden life in the Jewish quarters from Moscow to Casablanca. She is the very antithesis of the matriarchal Jewish mother of two generations ago. She passionately admires her mother who made the break and came to Palestine as a rebel against all this, who leaped from Europe's enclaves of Yiddish ways of life as it had existed for twenty centuries, to the sunny freedom of being a new woman in Galilee. For it must not be forgotten that her mother was not only a pioneer on the land, she was also a revolutionary who calmly exploded all the old concepts of love and marriage. And a double standard—one rigid sexual code for women, a pleasanter one for men—was something that she would never, never tolerate.

*   *   *

This, then, is the moral heritage of the sabra girl (except for those who are very religious.) Sex is quite free, even casual, among the young, although they have not reached the cool experimentation which seems to be the goal of young persons elsewhere. We offer no statistics on this subject, but as everywhere in the world today, sex seems to be more with us. In Israel it is not forbidden fruit; it is as available as oranges. Sabra take for granted their right to enjoy sex as naturally as they take for granted that the state of Israel exists. They have been brought up in a society which tacitly implies that what two people do in bed is their own affair.

Hebrew literature now includes *Fanny Hill*, the collected works of Henry Miller, and the dirty parts of Frank Harris. All these are in paperbacks, sold on newsstands, and avidly read. They are as much a part of the surroundings of the young Israeli as are Italian motorcycles and Japanese transistor radios and British pop records. They are the new appurtenances of youth, of a new one-world, teen-age subculture. As a result a youngster in Tel Aviv often has more in common with his contemporaries in New York and in Prague than he has with his own parents.

Except among the pious element of the population there is little discussion in the press about premarital sex, infidelity, and all the rest. We have interminable radio panels on juvenile delinquency, on what is wrong with youth today, but little hand wringing over sexual license. The battle for sexual freedom has been won. The sabra accepts this freedom matter-of-factly; he despises hypocrisy in all matters, refuses to be anything but ruthlessly honest in love, and is impatient of all the lying and pretending that usually goes with it.

This being Israel, where *politika* is on everybody's minds, the most popular Hebrew weekly, *Ha'olam Hazeh,* "This World," serves up a brisk mixture of politics and sex. On the front cover is invariably a posed nude, often blithely stolen from one of the American girlie magazines, and on the back cover, a devastating photograph of Dayan or whichever politico the editors are roasting that week. Similar magazines are often in trouble with the police because of their daring pictures, even though the editors indignantly claim that Israeli maidens besiege there offices for the honor of posing "like *Playboy.*"

The concept of virginity as a prized possession, except among the religious and "Oriental" communities, is vanishing. We certainly do not wish to imply that most Israelis are libertine. But we are living in a condoning age, termed permissive, and the sabras have acquired a direct, forthright approach to sex, as they have in all other matters of flesh and spirit. Still, many lumps have not yet dissolved in Israel's cauldron. We are unhomogenized. For example, the ultra-religious, some 15 per cent of the population, live rigid walled-in lives in which sex matters are conducted more or less as they have always been for two millenia. Rabbis thunder constantly about the depravity of our time and weep for the haughty daughters of Jerusalem who walk with outstreched necks. At the Jewish wedding ceremony the rabbi calls before him "the chaste virgin." At the funeral of an unmarried woman, regardless of age, the rabbi also mourns "the chaste virgin" on the presumption that if she had been anything less she would have long ago been stoned to death in the market place.

Among the immigrants from North Africa and other hot-blooded African lands the taboo on sex before marriage is still supreme. The old traditions are still very much alive here; on the wedding night the bride's mother will snatch up the bloody sheets and wave them aloft triumphantly before the cheering relatives who are congregated about; the groom's mother will search the bed for ketchup. Stabbings and murders of jealousy are common among these volatile newcomers; there are harrowing news stories about them every week right out of the pages of *Cavaleria Rusticana*. If a girl gets pregnant before being married off, her outraged brothers will often set fire to her with kerosene, to purge the family honor. These hair-raising occurrences happen with such monotonous regularity in Israel today that the stories are buried in the back pages of the press.

Abortions, though technically illegal, are freely available in Israel and are performed by the best gynocologists in the best hospitals. There is none of the traumatic nightmare of an abortion in America, and they are to be had a popular prices. If an unmarried woman decides to keep her child—as often happens today on the kibbutzim, and now and then in the towns—there is no *scandale,* only a buzzing, human curiosity as to who is the father.

Prostitution is a Latin-styled, highly emotional line of work in Israel, not as commercial a trade as it is elsewhere. The girls are mostly ignorant teen-agers from North African backgrounds, sabras and newcomers alike, callously seduced by pimps who well know that after this disgrace they will usually be driven from their homes.

*   *   *

It must be kept in mind that the girl on the banknote—the idealist with a rifle—represents less than half of the sabra girls in Israel today. She has little to do with the life and ambitions of many of the immigrant girls from the Muslim countries in Africa and Asia, the so-called "Orientals."

In Tel Aviv's great slum, called *Shunat Hatikva* (the "Neighborhood of Hope," as the poetic first settlers called it), families of eight or ten "Oriental Jews" crammed into one or two rooms are common. This results, predictably, in the youth from these homes fleeing into a blind alley of petty holdups, minor black marketeering, and semiprofessional prostitution.

Besides the vicissitudes of such an environment, the girls have to put up with the venerable Middle East custom, wherein the male head of the house puts his wife or wives to work at once; and waits impatiently for his children to reach an age when they can also go to work—say at ten or twelve—thus enabling the patriarch to live out his days in a life of dignity and honor, smoking water pipes and playing *sheshbesh* in the local café.

Now the girls from these homes are not at all like the girl on the banknote. They drop out of school; their pride and hopes, they believe, are trampled upon, and they often mock the sabra values of idealism and all that Israel stands for. They go to American films every night, spend every cent on clothes and pop records, and carry pictures of Elvis Presley in their purses. Many of them claim to despise Israel, blame the "European Jews" for all their troubles, and would leave tomorrow for Paris or New York if they could manage it, which they cannot. They remain, not in, not out, of the Israeli establishment, and are caught with a love-hate ambivalence toward the image of the dedicated, idealistic sabra.

Yet the image on the banknote remains our national pin-up girl. She is what most of us would like our own daughters to be. We ourselves may be grubbing to get that pleasantly posh villa in Herzlia, but we like to picture our girls standing guard along the Negev or on the Heights of Golan, which she does, of course, during her army service from the age of eighteen or twenty. Then she usually steps down from the role of pioneer-defender, and does her best to get that villa in Herzlia herself, preferably with a car of her own. Off duty, between wars so to say, she lays down her rifle.

But the world never forgets her rifle. It is inseparable from her person in the modern sexual fantasy that has made the sabra girl internationally famous. Without plunging too deeply into the subterranean maze of Freudian thought, it is a fact that throughout history Jewish women have always evoked a certain image in the folklore of Christian lust. They arouse the dark passions. The Gentile believes the Jewess to be sensual and fiery and as overripe as the race itself. He feels that her flesh has lost its innocence from birth; that the long experience and ancient secrets of the race are in her overbearing breasts and knowing haunches.

And there is more. There is the symbolism of black desires and evil satisfactions that he would not dare perform upon his own pallid women. This is not far removed from the lust and the appeal to sadistic urges that the symbol of the naked Negro woman suggests and excites; the dark flesh of the slave girl who cannot resist, whom the white master may enjoy and violate as he pleases.

"One of the elements of [the anti-Semite's] hatred is a profound sexual attraction toward Jews," Jean-Paul Satre has written. "His behavior reflects a curiosity fascinated by Evil, but above all, I think, it represents a basic sadism.

"There is in the words 'a beautiful Jewess' a very special sexual significance, one quite different from that contained in the words 'beautiful Roumanian,' 'beautiful Greek,' or 'beautiful American,' for example. This phrase carries an aura of rape and massacre. The 'beautiful Jewess' is she whom the Cossacks under the czars dragged by her hair through the streets of her burning village. . . . Frequently violated or beaten, she sometimes succeeds in escaping dishonor by means of death, but that is a form of justice. . . . I think nothing more is needed to indicate the place the Jewess holds as a sexual symbol in folklore." *

Now in our curious age, many observers are convinced that women have become more aggressive, masculine, and that men have become more passive, feminine. Could it be that the sabra girl with the rifle plays a unique role in modern sexual fantasy precisely because she has reversed the role of the "violated and beaten Jewess," because she has suddenly sprung up as a powerful, Gentile-subduing Jewess? She stands for an end to the long calvary of the Jew, of an end to Jewish subjection, but does she perhaps also excite with a special fascination and a special appeal to fantasy—the aroused Huntress who wields the all-conquering Freudian symbol of the gun?

* Jean-Paul Sartre, *Anti-Semite and Jew*. Schocken Books, 1948. The reader may recall a fictional treatment of all this in Robert Briffault's brilliant novel, *Europa*.

CHAPTER X

The Thorns of the Sabra: Chutzpah

✡   Chutzpah: Insolence, audacity, cheek, impudence, impertinence, effrontery, gall.
"Chutzpah pays even against heaven."

—The Talmud

One of the bemusing social revolutions of the jet age is the annual flight of northern women heading south. A century ago only the very rich and very bold gentlewoman was able to seek out the wilder shores of love, the hot climates where men were men, imperious, masterful males who tamed a high-spirited woman as easily as they rode a quivering mare.

Today, chartered planes twice daily deliver Swedish girls to the Greek demigods of Rhodes; hot-blooded Spanish cavaliers have been embraced by English ladies; American secretaries wander through Florence and Venice in lonely search for a bitter but fascinating Italian, who will lay his soul bare in an antique shop.

In the past decade, Israel has attracted more and more women traveling alone. They come for the sun, the Holy Places, and to observe the natives. Our young men are taller than the Greeks, less preening than the Italians, more cultured than the Spanish. They are often bronzed, purposeful types right off the pages of *Exodus*.

A remarkable number of young women (Gentiles as well as Jews) come for an extended vacation, or for six months or a year, "to give Israel a try." Many of them are recently divorced, or are fleeing unhappiness. Israel seems the answer to their personal problems. Besides, they always wanted to "do something" for Israel. They know that life in Israel is affirmative, up-beat; and it's far, far away from wherever they came from.

It sounds exciting, and it is. You can work on a kibbutz half-day to pay your keep, and the rest of the time is your own. If you prefer, you can spend your time in town, sitting in the outdoor cafés and watching the world go by. Life is delightfully casual, and Israel is "one big family." You can saunter about alone, wherever you please, without fear of aggressive incidents (but keep away from the borders). You can be disdainfully poor, and dress in khaki trousers or in sexy rolled-up bloomers, the way the sabra girls do. And you can meet one of those Tarzans with an M.A. almost anywhere. It seems that a girl can have quite a vacation.

That is how it looks from far away. Upon closer contact, however, our girl discovers a rather prickly, repellant side to the sabra—his *chutzpah*. This indispensable word in Hebrew means cheek, gall, brazen nerve, or effrontery.

Our innocent girl arrives at Lydda Airport overloaded with three suitcases. She has brought severely simple clothes, she has read two books on the Six Days' War, and even three chapters of Israel's complex Nobel Prize novelist, Agnon. She has acquired views on America's suicidal policy in the Middle East, Jewish novelists, the New Left, and What To Do With The Arab Refugees. She is ready for a Meaningful Experience.

She and her bags are dumped unceremoniously at a taxi stand by a sweating porter. She is about to throw herself wearily into the back seat when a young man appears out of nowhere and beats her to it. "This is my cab!" she cries. "I was here before you," the young man answers curtly. "I just went to get cigarettes." She appeals to him silently with her eyes, glancing at her luggage. The young man settles himself indifferently in the back, opens his newspaper, and the taxi speeds off. Welcome to Israel, she says to herself, cursing his impudence, his chutzpah.

At the hotel, everyone looked over fifty. The next day she dutifully joined a busload of tourists and was whisked about from one model settlement to another. She was sticky and bored, and all the other passengers were elderly Zionists from a half dozen lands, making the trip of a lifetime to the Promised Land. The guide looked at her disapprovingly as she yawned when he repeated for the third time how thirty years ago this remarkable cluster of concrete houses had been a malarial desert. Our girl sighed and wondered where all these romantic sabras could be found. It seemed as though the bus would never get back to the hotel.

That night there was a presentation of Israeli folk dances in the hotel lobby, for tourists too decrepit or too lazy to seek out the real thing for themselves. Prepackaged tourist entertainment she just couldn't take tonight, and she asked the clerk at the desk where she might witness some real hora dancing. He looked doubtful. In Tel Aviv, madame? He saw her disappointment, and added kindly, "Why don't you take a stroll on Dizengoff Road? It's very gay at night. That's where all the *nachtleben* is, and the young people."

Sure enough, Dizengoff Road seemed intriguing with smart shops set between a continuous row of outdoor cafés. For block after block, she beheld a sea of faces, young, carefree people sitting around miniscule tables, all jostled together in an incredibly crowded fashion. Our girl looked at them all wistfully. Pangs of loneliness overwhelmed her. It was worse than being lonely in New York—there she took unhappiness for granted.

She paused before one café that seemed to attract a rather Bohemian, raffish-looking cilentele. She would have liked to sit down, but there wasn't an empty place to be had. Suddenly she saw a hand waving at her, and a grinning face was attached to it. It was the young man who had grabbed her taxi at the airport. He was sitting at a table with three other young men. "Shalom!" he called. "Come on over."

She felt herself steaming up. Now that's the limit, she thought furiously. He doesn't even bother to stand up, let alone come over, and he has the *chutzpah* to expect me to join him.

"Don't you remember me?" he called across a dozen noisy tables, "At the airport. You wanted to steal my taxi."

"I remember you all right," she called back, as witheringly as she could manage. She stood there on the sidewalk uncertainly, aware of fifty pairs of curious eyes upon her. Was she really carrying on a shouted conversation in public with a stranger?

"So pull up a chair," the young man half-shouted. He pointed with his head to a dark passageway next to the café. She looked there and saw an enormous pile of fold-up chairs stacked together. "What are you waiting for?"

Her mind revolted, but her body walked toward the stack of chairs. He *was* handsome, damn it, she thought. She grappled with the pile, and managed to extract one chair after a few tugs. Nobody bothered to move aside as she wove toward the young man's table with the chair in her hands. She was burning with humiliation for letting herself be ordered around. It's all a lark, she argued with herself. It would make a droll story to tell the girls back at the office.

She stood before his table, and he nudged over a bit to make room for her to unfold the chair and put it next to his. He introduced himself as Uzi. "This is Dov, Shmuel, and Gingi." The other three young men grunted in surly recognition.

Uzi asked her how she liked Israel. "Have you come to settle here?" She replied that she was just on vacation. He seemed to lose interest after that, half-turned and resumed his conversation with his friends. It was in Hebrew, of course, and she sat there like a dummy, getting more furious every moment. Sabras, she thought. The rudest people on earth. First he insults her by making her struggle alone with that damn chair, and then he turns his back and ignores her. She was just about to tell him off and leave, when he swung around to her and said, "Would you care to go to a movie?"

It was an American film. Doris Day spent an hour in bed protecting her virginity against her boy friend. Uzi groaned, and kept making pained remarks. "Garbage *Americai*," he announced. "Why do you keep making this nonsense? The world is in flames, and this is all you Americans got to worry about."

She secretly agreed with him, and she wouldn't have been caught dead at a Doris Day film back home, but now she felt a curious patriotic surge. "It's just family entertainment," she said weakly. "Entertainment," he said, and rose abruptly. "Let's get out of here before I puke." He might have asked her if she cared to leave, she thought, following him. Oh no, not the almighty sabra.

The film had put him in an accusing mood. "You Americans. Burning babies in Viet Nam and feeding the world pap like this. What kind of a lunatic people are you, anyway?"

That was too much. She replied heatedly that millions of Americans, including herself, were against the Viet Nam war, and nobody forced him to go to a Doris Day film if he didn't want to. She told him that she herself devoted all her free time to civil rights. Somehow she didn't sound convincing. They walked along and she found herself personally responsible for the American Way of Life, as exemplified by police dogs in Alabama, Mayor Daley in Chicago, and kids growing up hooked on TV and pot.

He didn't seem impressed with her arguments about how radical much of America was. He paused before a restaurant. "Let's eat," he said gloomily.

She followed him inside. Arab style, she thought, the lord and master two paces ahead of his woman. It was an exotic place in the Yemenite quarter, with the walls painted blue against the Evil Eye. It was jammed with Israelis, there wasn't a tourist in sight, and she told herself that at least she was being taken to the real thing.

"Try some real Yemenite food," he said, and ordered humus and tchina for them both.

"I tried it last night," she said. "I can't stand it."

"Don't be silly," he insisted. "It's delicious. Wait till you taste the way they make it here."

It tasted awful, all oily and smelly. And it didn't help to watch Uzi eat with gusto and swill his bread around with his fingers, Arab style.

Suddenly Dov and Shmuel and Gingi appeared, and without as much as a *shalom* to her slumped down at their table. They started talking rapidly in Hebrew and she was out in the cold again. The place was terribly noisy and she was getting a headache. The odor of the Levantine food turned her stomach, and she felt wretched.

Uzi glanced at her. "You look awful," he said critically. "I'd better take you home." "Thanks for the compliment," she snapped. They walked in silence along the half-lit streets. He stopped, and she saw him looking at her, and he came closer. *He wouldn't dare,* she thought, and then he was trying to kiss her.

She shoved him away. "Really," she said coldly, "That's the limit."

He stared at her uncomprehendingly, then shrugged. *"Lo rotzah, lo tszarich,"* he said cheerfully. "Old sabra saying. You don't want to, you don't have to."

He left her in front of her hotel. She could hear him whistling as he walked away.

Upstairs, she laid down on her bed and closed her eyes. It had been without doubt the most miserable evening she had ever had. Even his just walking away was an insult. And the least he could have done was try to kiss her again.

She was so upset she couldn't sleep, and she wrote a long letter to her girl friend Judy in New York, very amusing, making it all sound arch, and herself the poised, knowing traveler. My dear, these sabras are so cocky, they're so sure they know everything, that God chose them personally, and they treat their women like Arab squaws, or whatever they were called. She added wryly that she was longing for the gallant, considerate American men they had both deplored as too submissive, and would probably fall into the arms of the first one she met.

Two days later she was amazed when Uzi rang up and invited her to a party. She was even more amazed to hear herself accept. When he picked her up, she let him have it with both barrels. "I suppose you're going to be as insufferably rude as you were last time. I never heard of such chutzpah."

"Who me?" he looked at her in astonishment. "Chutzpah? Don't talk like an idiot."

"First you hog my taxi—"

"It was my turn, damn it. We don't prostrate ourselves before a woman in this country. What are you, pregnant? Or a war invalid?"

"Then you let me fetch my own chair at the café."

"It wasn't so heavy. You want to be treated like a painted doll? We are not *decadenti*, like you Americans. I was honoring you, you nitwit, and treating you like a comrade."

"I assume you were honoring me when you told me I looked terrible."

"We say what we think," he exploded. *"Yashar l'inyan—*straight to the point. We don't go in for hypocrisy and false smiles all the time. If I tell you when you look awful, you'll believe me when I say you look great. We treat our girls as comrades, and are truthful with them."

She was silent a moment. "I suppose you'll ignore me at the party, and everyone will be rude again and speak Hebrew around me."

"If I want to talk to my pals, I talk to them. If you want them to speak English, show them you're interested in their conversation. Don't expect them to fall all over you, just because you're a pretty *girl!"*

The party was made up of two dozen young Israelis standing about a room, ignoring the French rock-and-roll on the phonograph. Sure enough, Uzi's three buddies were there. Sure enough, he left her alone, and went to talk to their hostess. She walked over to where the drinks were, and poured her own glass of wine. Then she joined two good-looking chaps deep in conversation, and said in her clipped, executive-secretary voice, "Do you mind speaking English? I'm really terribly interested."

"With pleasure," the tall one beamed, and she listened to a demolishing critique of a new Israeli film, and a position paper on how to handle El Fatah. She asked intelligent questions, and they explained earnestly, and offered to get her some background reading material. They asked her about the student riots in America, and listened attentively as she sketched the background.

Uzi showed up with a plate of humus and tchina. He smiled at her, and she smiled back, and the humus tasted not bad at all.

It was a marvelous evening. One of the boys started playing a guitar, and they all sat in a circle on the floor and sang Israeli folksongs. After a while, Gingi, Uzi's friend, came up to her and in fumbling English apologized for not talking to her until now. He was ashamed of his English, he said, and always embarrassed when he had to speak it, but he could read Dylan Thomas without the aid of a dictionary. She was ashamed with herself for having thought him rude, and got along fine with Gingi. She asked him why he and Uzi and Dov and Shmuel were always together. "Are you brothers or something?"

"We used to be five," he said, "with Moshe." "We're in the same tank battalion, and are called up together every time there's trouble. It gets to be a habit to stick together."

"Where is the fifth?" she asked.

"Moshe was hit while giving us cover. In the Six Days' War. Uzi crawled over a Syrian tank that was blazing away, and dragged Moshe out of there. Moshe died in Uzi's arms on the way to the hospital."

When Uzi took her back to the hotel that night, her eyes were moist as she returned his kiss, and she rode down through the Negev with him that weekend, on the back of his *Vespa* motorcycle, hugging his waist as the sun and wind blew strongly against her, and they climbed Masada together and she listened humbly as he explained how the Jews had fought off the Romans and then killed themselves with pride and dignity rather than surrender.

She stopped wearing make-up, and went around in rolled-up shorts, and got a wonderful tan, and was delighted when someone mistook her for a sabra. When it was time to go home, she thought with a sinking heart of the men she knew whose only worry was whether they were going to make it to the two-car homes and the barbecue pits. She cabled for another two weeks' leave, and wrote an ecstatic letter to Judy on how life was vibrant and meaningful in Israel. The men were marvelous, virile, *y'shar l'inyan,* straight to the point. They didn't waste an evening on all the trite nonsense that men chattered in New York. They were new Jews with pride and dignity, a little brusque, but that was because they faced life unflinchingly. They treated a woman like a comrade. There was nobody like the sabras.

* * *

"Horror stories" about the chutzpah of the sabra—men, women, and children alike—are notorious. What appears to be (and often is) their cheek, their insolence, has shocked and enraged everyone who has met them. Sabras freely admit their chutzpah as a people, but are rarely aware of being chutzpadik themselves. They will tell you, "Oh, we're terrible. It's a national vice. I am not so bad, but I have some very rude friends."

But what is a national vice began as a pioneer virtue. Our passionate utopians wanted Palestine to become the laboratory of daring social experiments. The kibbutz was to be "the freest society in the world." You said what you thought, and not what was considered polite. You did what you thought was right, with British "bloody-mindedness," and stuck to your beliefs no matter how unpopular they were. The kibbutz discussion meetings were (and still are), all-out battles in which you said what you damn well thought of your neighbor, because his work and conduct affected the well-being of all the comrades within the commune. There was no time, no place for frivolities, empty polite gestures, artificial manners. They had emerged from the ghetto to the sun at noon and they would face life honestly. Thus was born chutzpah.*

Our story has suggested that it is our young men who are afflicted with chutzpah, but our girls are just as dismayingly brazen.

It was the girls who fought tooth and nail for equality and comradeship between the sexes. All this was around 1910. The kibbutz idea had not as yet evolved. The boys who dreamed of a *productivi* life on the land formed labor platoons and hired themselves out to the well-to-do Jewish planters. The girls, however, could not find work, except as maids; the old-fashioned planters refused to hire women as laborers, and were aghast at the idea of nice Jewish girls sweating under the sun. But the girls were adamant. They had the chutzpah to disguise themselves in men's trousers, and worked in the orange groves alongside their men. Such a proud tradition dies hard.

Today, when a young Israeli maiden says what she thinks in England or in America, it is often a social disaster. She will tell her American uncle that the German Jews felt secure, too, and look what happened to them. She will listen to a London family rhapsodize about Israel, and how valiantly they toil for the Zionist cause in London; and then she will say, "If you're all such big Zionists, why on earth don't you live in Israel?"

---

* The all-seeing Bruno Bettelheim, the famous educator, is one of the few foreign observers who has sensed the true nature of the sabra's chutzpah. In his recent book, *Children of the Dream*, he writes: "Here is a rejection, in the kibbutz, of all emotionalism as being reminiscent of the ghetto. In its place is a desire for authenticity. And this is expressed through language by an avoidance of what we would consider politeness. . . . I found kibbutzniks so direct, with each other and with me, that it seemed a deliberate stance of shunning all efforts to soften bluntness, whether by politeness or by any other way of making their statements more acceptable to the other person.

"Thus, while their language stresses honestly and directness more than politeness, the reasons for it are doubly determined."

Everywhere abroad she encounters incidents that confirm what she has been taught about the *decadenti* life with its warped values. In London's Marks and Spencer the salesgirl calls her luv, at Macy's in New York they call her honey. It's all so false, so hypocritical. No sabra would ever talk like that. It is true, as the teacher said, that the women in the Diaspora (the awful world of Exile outside of Israel) wear false eyelashes and blonde wigs and dresses designed to round off their bottoms. They just ogle and wiggle their way through life, instead of being real human beings. It is true that all the men have grim faces and wear pompous suits and neckties even in the heat, and rush about buying and selling, instead of living *productivi* lives in a meaningful socialist society. The sabra feels sorry for them. She is glad she lives on a kibbutz, where nobody needs money at all.

Ironically, what began as a new vision of human equality persists as an offensive behavior pattern. The noble cause of comradeship between the sexes has been won, and is taken for granted, but chutzpah remains as an Israel life style. Our young sabra children are the worst offenders; they have grown up hearing their parents' blunt speech, and have enthusiastically adopted it themselves. You will rarely hear a sabra child say "Thank you" or "Please." His despairing parents cry, "Did you ever see such chutzpah? He's a real sabra."

Chutzpah is alarmingly close to chauvinism, and it must be admitted that the sabra is usually passionately chauvinistic in an era when no gospel has been more discredited in the West than blind, excessive patriotism. Most of the world shudders at the tribal self-idealization so much admired just a while ago—"My country right or wrong," "Rule, Britannia," and all the other slogans that led to jingoism. We want to hang onto our necks, without any slogans at all. Morally, most of us are internationalists. Our young wish to be as universal as blades of grass.

But the young Israeli cannot afford this, and will tell you defensively, "After all, you can't build a nation without nationalism." But there is a deeper reason, perhaps for his chauvinism: the innbred, self-congratulatory Jewish sense of superiority. Real or imagined, this superiority always infuriated the gentile. Denied a homeland, vilified, the Jew turned his vision inward and fed on his spiritual arrogance. He huddled in ghettos and rejoiced in his four thousand years of apartness, of uniqueness.

Today, the sabra learns at an early age that Jerusalem, for ancient and medieval scholars, was the umbilicus of the universe, and that for a thousand years all maps were designed with Jerusalem placed in the honored center. The Old Testament, which the sabra adores, is a saga based upon a sensationally ultrachauvinistic event and premise: The Lord of the Universe entered into solemn pact with Abraham, saying, "I will establish my covenant between Me and thee and thy seed after thee in their generations for an everlasting covenant."

As a sign of this sacred bond, of being special seed, Chosen, The Lord of the Universe commands Abraham: "Every man child among you shall be circumcized. And ye shall circumcize the flesh of your foreskin; and it shall be a token of the covenant between you and Me."

Today, the sabra solemnly circumcizes his man child, eight days after it is born, as a proud badge of being apart, marked as the Chosen of God. The sabra may be ungodly himself, but he would not dream of breaking this mystic ritual that has passed from father to son since the Jews began.

After having learned that the children of Abraham are chosen above all the nations, the sabra learns that he himself is indeed chosen above all Jews. He learns that between 1880 and the outbreak of World War I, some three million Jews fled from the persecutions of eastern Europe. The majority of them sought the fleshpots of America and other Exiles; only fifty thousand, the elite of Jewry, ventured unto the desert and swampland of Palestine to be born again New Jews. He learns that the world is divided into two distinct areas: the Land of Israel on the one hand, and the Diaspora, the lands of Jewish Exile, on the other.

All revolutionary movements are by definition chauvinistic: our cause is the splendid true cause, and well worth dying for. We have a Mission, and are about to recover our true selves which bondage has caked with filth. We do not have indoor toilets, but we are self-denying, we are pure, and we are the salt of the earth. If we seem arrogant, very well, we are arrogant. You try living the spartan life that we do, and see if you can take it without becoming self-righteous and bitter and vindictive.

In Israel, this "revolutionary chauvinism" has been heightened by the idea of there being something exalted about dwelling in a corner of the world called Israel. This chauvinistic notion is imbedded in the very language of the sabra, Hebrew. An immigrant is an *oleh*, "one who goes up" to Zion, presumably in a state of elevation. A settler who chucks it all and departs for less harsher shores is a *yored* "one who goes down." And there are fewer more derogatory epithets in the wrathful Hebrew tongue than *yored;* it seethes with scathing denunciation and shame for him who forgets Jerusalem the Golden and abandons the tenets of righteousness.

A *yored,* whatever his other qualities may be, is damned forever. Theodore Bikel came to Palestine as a young refugee from Central Europe. He spent some ten years in the country before going on to seek his fortune in America, where he became an eminent and internationally admired folk singer. His name came up recently in a conversation in Tel Aviv. "Who?" inquired an old kibbutznik, "Bikel? Oh yes, I remember now. That *yored.*"

The sabra's chauvinism toward Jews "in exile" is very real. This is because of the Zionist ideal itself. The basic tenets of Zionism can be crudely sketched as follows: All the Jews throughout the world are one nation. Jews need their own state, to which all Jews will flock sooner or later, either of their own will, or driven by inevitable persecution.

Nothing of the kind occurred, of course. Most of the world's Jews have not come to Israel, despite the awesome vow, "If I forget Thee, O Jerusalem," and despite the toast still universally made by Jews during the feast of Passover, "Next year in Jerusalem!"

All this rubs against the sabra's common sense. He knows that you do not have to tear your clothes in lamentation for Zion anymore. There are planes leaving every day. All you have to do is to buy a ticket and get over here.

This plain truth has led to much embarrassment on the part of Jews outside Israel who enjoy intoning, "Yea, we wept when we remembered Zion," and who now find excellent reasons for not dwelling in Zion. The sabra ironically observes all this and accounts for the complex, ambivilant, and highly emotional relationship between the sabra and the American Jew. Tens of thousands of young Israelis have studied in Amreica, and any American who has met them will tell you, "Israel is a great country, but boy, those snot-nosed sabras. They're so damned superior, so cocky, so full of *chutzpah.* They think they know everything and have nothing to learn."

But ironically, it is usually the sabra's same *chutzpah,* even *chauvinism,* that moves the American to support him with devotion and cash. As James Yaffe shrewdly observes in his book *The American Jews,* "the American Jew sees Israel as a vicarious extension of himself. By identifying with those bronzed invincible heroes, he somehow takes on some of the bravery, some of the strength, that he feels he could never possess otherwise. There is a strong strain of magic in this—the superstitious magic of primitive people who believe that by drinking the tiger's blood or wearing his skin they can assume the characteristics of the tiger."

The sabra is well aware of this American admiration, and it heightens his chauvinistic feelings. Also, along with ecstatic praise for such technological triumphs as Apollo 11, the sabra's newspapers are filled with accounts of an America that sometimes seems to resemble the last weeks of the Roman Empire. Crime-ridden streets, hunger, brutal police, student riots, drug addiction, and sex mania preoccupy the dissolute populace, and their bumbling statesmen are pushovers for the cool, ruthlessly Russian strategists. He reads *Playboy* at his barber's, with its fantasies of the pad, the hi-fi, the more than willing beauties, the poised, affluent, sexcrazed young swinger, and thinks, this is the people who have the atomic bomb.

He has seen the fast-buck exploitations of his Six Days' War which were sold in America as cartoon and joke books, with titles such as "Israel's Funniest Hour." He cannot believe their vulgarity. He reads some of the cartoons: "What are the Israelis going to call the Suez Canal? Miami Beach East." He reads another: A gay Israeli soldier says to his officer, "After we conquer the Suez Canal, do we get to eat lox?"

The sabra understands the crass self-glorification of the American Jew during the sabra's grim war. But he wonders if the Americans are really so mad as to link the savage fighting in Sinai, and on the Golan Heights, with Miami Beach and lox. This may be hilarious humor in America, but the sabra fought too bloodily himself, and had too many comrades killed or maimed, to be amused. Instead, it makes him depressed, and impells a *chutzpahdik* response.

But hopefully, chutzpah and chauvinism will diminish

when Israel becomes a more peaceful place. To a large extent, the sabra's ways are but the curt brusqueness of the frontiersman whose life is uncertain and perilous. Unlike the Arabs, who love grandiloquent words, he is impatient with those who talk and talk. Unlike the Italians, he has no need to adorn his life with bravura and fabricated drama. Life for the sabra is dramatic enough within Fortress Israel. And as long as it remains that way, he needs all the chutzpah he can muster.

CHAPTER XI

On Husbands, Wives, and Rabbis

✡   "Blessed be the Lord, King of the Universe, for not creating me
a woman."
>   —Daily morning prayer of a pious Jewish
>   male

"Blessed be the Lord, King of the Universe, Who created me
according to His Will."
>   —Daily morning prayer of a pious Jewish
>   female

In Israel, today, a wife is still called by the lowly, pejorative
term that the Old Testament calls her: *isha*, woman. Her
husband is still addressed by his splendid biblical title, *ba'al*,
master. In the glorious days of the Kings of Israel, upon marriage an *isha* became the physical possession, the chattel, of
her *ba'al*, along with his handmaidens and slaves, his ox and
his ass. For this reason, "to marry a wife" and "to become
master" have the same root meanings in Hebrew. The in-
finitive *liv'ol*, commonly used in the sacred texts, means
bluntly, and most vulgarly, to possess a woman sexually.

What our fiercely free sabra girl thinks of referring to her
husband a dozen times a day as "my master," with all the
humiliating connotations described above, may well be imag-

ined by the reader. Many wives (the coauthor of this book included) often cannot bring themselves to utter the phrase without embarrassment. Whenever possible they get around it by saying "my man," or on the kibbutz, "my comrade."

Thus we behold the not always amusing situation of the modern Israeli, still wandering in a bronze-age petrified forest, surrounded by the dead trunks of an incredibly ancient, incredibly codified tradition. Four thousand years is a long, long time.

How fares our Huntress, the sabra girl with a gun, when confronted with marriage? Does she shrink from the thought of legally becoming an *isha?* To convey some idea of what this involves, we must discuss the Rabbinical Courts. There is no such thing as a civil wedding in Israel (although, ironically, in bibilcal days marriage was a secular, nonreligious ceremony); no matter if you vote Left or eat pork on Yom Kippur, the rabbis have got you if you want to get married.

Until their fairly recent removal to more elegant quarters, the Rabbinical Court of Tel Aviv stood on a squalid street and was notorious for its gloomy, peeling corridors in which you arranged your personal destiny. Balzac would have loved this place. At eight in the morning the seamy reception hall was already jammed with couples. Flies buzzed everywhere. A dank odor of sweat and urine hung over the steaming hall. Here one beheld a fascinating microcosm of Israel: wiry Yemenites, burly Poles, brilliantined North Africans, blonde Hollanders, nut-brown Indians, Americans in jeans, with Camus in their hip pockets—all Jews.

There were two queues in the hall, leading to adjacent doors. Over one, a sign read, "Registration of Marriages," over the other door, "Applications for Divorce." Here the human comedy was endlessly enacted. In the divorce queue, a worn-out mother straight out of Daumier unconcernedly suckles an infant at her breast, scolds her three brats who are darting about, and in a frenzied voice relates to one and all the perfidy of her husband.

In the marriage queue an intense young man surveys disdainfully the men in the divorce queue, with an expression that clearly says, "This will never happen to me." His eyes are met with a weary and cynical appraisal from the divorce queue, "The hell it won't."

In the courtyard outside, a half-dozen weddings are being simultaneously performed, on a treadmill basis, for those in a hurry to get it over with, and for those without funds for a private wedding. The traditional wedding canopies jostle together like square beach unmbrellas, with each bride and groom bunched in by rabbis and ministrants, relatives, and well-wishers. The din never ceases, and the rabbis half shout to be heard as they chant the ritual.

Under one canopy, an orthodox young man, with the wan face of a religious scholar, tremblingly lifts the veil of his bride and beholds her for the first time in his life. A gray-haired, stooped couple clasp hands tightly as the rabbi repeats the age-old vows, and you notice the blue tattoed numbers of the Nazi concentration camp on their forearms. A swarthy, belligerent workman in workboots makes no attempt to hide his contempt for the proceedings and glances impatiently at his watch, calculating the lost work hours this bourgeois mumbo jumbo is costing him. Not fifteen minutes elapse before a scurrying, harassed rabbinical clerk shouts, "Move along now. Next couple!"

In another wing of the building sadder ceremonies are being enacted. Here, a *ba'al* repudiates his *isha,* flings his marriage certificate on the floor, and intones three times, "I cast thee off, I cast thee off, I cast thee off." He is thereupon divorced. An *isha,* however, if her *ba'al* refuses his consent, can almost never obtain a divorce without years of petitioning.

*   *   *

Is our sabra dragged protestingly into his archaic arena? Does she long for the carefree ways of her mother's day, when a pioneer girl in Galilee loved deeply, and when love passed was her own mistress again?

Not a bit. She has seen enough suffering as the result of nonmarriage unions and may have herself suffered as a child from its lack of stability. She wants to get married and stay married—and with a bang-up wedding, mind you—rabbi, white dress, orchestra, the lot. She knows that, life being as it is, after a few years she may take a lover, but she will be a secure married woman, and she will try not to rock the marital boat too much.

Her longing for the legal tie is all the more bemusing when one recalls that in the 1930's, among the staunchly atheist kibbutzim, a settlement would be visited twice a year by an old rabbi. Strapped to his donkey would be a makeshift *chupah,* or wedding canopy. Often, the only brides who stepped under the *chupah* were girls seven months gone, who agreed to a wedding for the sake of the child.

The Big Change in our notions about marriage has been successfully caught by the Israeli humorist, Ephraim Kishon, in his play *The Wedding Certificate*—the smash Israeli comedy hit over the last twenty years. Middle-aged ex-pioneer couples of course never bothered to get married. Today, father is a prosperous Tel Aviv businessman. Daughter is about to be married to a snotty son-in-law, who casually asks to see the wedding certificate of the parents of his betrothed. All kinds of high jinks ensue, making fun of the new propriety on our once-bohemian land.

It must be admitted that with marriage our sabra girl

sheds much of her glamor. Superficially, she is now not much different from a young married in Holland or Hungary. She dreams of a little house, a ruinously taxed television set, and she usually hates housework. She much prefers to leave the house and go to work in the morning, even though a part-time maid eats up much of her salary.

Men in Israel admire their wives as *persons*. There is more shared comradeship than when a London husband drives home after a hard day in the city, or a Larchmont wife meets her spouse on the 5:37 out of Grand Central Station in New York. It is the mutual respect, say, known to the American pioneers of the West, when the determined wife drove the horses, used a gun, and protected her brood within the stockade at night. Fortress Israel still is one large stockade.

And a young wife holds her husband differently in her arms in a land where men are called up on army reserve training one or two months out of every year, where the sound of a motorcycle and a rap at the door at midnight may mean that it looks like war again, and the army messenger has come to tell your husband to be at his unit's usual rendezvous point by dawn.

Sexually speaking, the marital ties between husband and wife are not tightly woven for many sabras. When your wife is your comrade, and shares your dangers, it is not easy to deny her your own little relaxations and pleasures.

In this connection, it is instructive to glance at Jewish tradition concerning the flesh and the devil. As every prurient schoolboy knows, the Old Testament fairly seethes with sex (and violence too, for that matter—a fact usually overlooked by those disturbed by our own violence today.)

The creation of the first two human beings implies that monogamous marriage is the will of God; polygamy first appears in the notorious line of Cain, when Lamek takes two wives. Of the Ten Commandments, no less than three deal with conduct between husband and wife.

Yet the patriarch's generous view of what is monogamy—for the male—would raise eyebrows in most societies today. Jewish kings had harems. Desire is clearly viewed as the natural way of flesh. To take a second wife may be frowned upon, but for a man to sleep with his concubines, hand-maidens, and slaves who fill his tents is not merely tolerated but, as far as the present writers can make out, unremarkable and entirely expected.

An *isha*, of course, was forbidden such excursions. Her fornication with anyone was "the great sin," punishable by disgrace and death. Nothing is known of the sexual behavior expected of the unmarried woman; we know only that a priest's daughter who became a prostitute was to be burned alive. (Leviticus 21: 9.)

But no moral perdition faced a *ba'al*, unless he left his own tents and violated the property rights of another *ba'al* by taking his neighbor's wife. This was a very grave matter indeed. The sages of Israel sensibly considered the sin of adultery as applying when one takes carnally not merely another woman, but a *married* woman. This vital distinction of property rights has been slurred over by endless generations of Christian preachers, grappling with the serpent, who repeat the thunderous injunction: Thou shalt not commit adultery. The Protestant ethic has preferred to ignore the fact that the ancient Jews regarded sexual congress as normal, enjoyable, and not at all abhorrent, unless it disturbs the tranquillity of the tribe.

Thus we see the Israelite male enjoying what may be termed a relative monogamy, with his sexual appetite and restlessness fully provided for within his own tents, and risking stoning to death only if he ventured beyond to "the strange woman," one's neighbor's wife. The willingness of one's neighbor's wife is clearly noted in the last collection of Proverbs, which warns the upright young man against seduction by a wanton wife who is ready to betray her *ba'al.*

When the walls of the Temple crumbled before Rome, and the Jews were scattered to the four corners of the earth, they required a new code of conduct in the foreign lands. This they developed in the Talmud, which interpreted the ancient Mosaic concepts for a Jew in a pagan world. The Talmud, with its 613 precepts, guided the daily life of the pious Jew for the next two thousand years.

The relative monogamy of the patriarchs was out, of course; Jews no longer had concubines and handmaidens. Women were still judged by nature sinful, but a man's desire for them was not sinful. "God does nothing without a deliberate purpose, and as he gave man sexual organs and desire, the exercise of them must be good." But only with one's wife, and at the proper time.

In the *shtetls,* the small towns and enclaves in which Jews lived, from the eastern border of Germany to the western side of Czarist Russia, the purity of home life was reinforced by separating the daily routine of men and women. A personal God was a living reality in the *shtetl,* and study of the Holy Books the only real occupation of a man. (An eager grandfather would test his young grandson for first signs of intellectual promise.) Women disturbed. A woman's body too freely contemplated would fill a scholar with lustful thoughts, and mar his pondering of the sacred books.

The burning of the flesh was faced with utter practicality: boys, in particular promising students, were married off very young, so that their bodies would be at peace. "There are no Jewish monasteries" runs an old Jewish proverb. Elaborate precautions were taken against the temptations of "the strange woman"; a woman's hair was cut off when she became a bride, and she wore a covering or wig for the rest of her days on earth, to reduce the spell of her dangerous charms. Ultra-orthodox brides in Israel today still are shorn—sabras included.

A woman was forbidden to wear short sleeves in the presence of men who were studying the Talmud; the sight of her bare flesh could make a man swoon. To this day, among pious Jews of Israel, a man will not look directly at a woman, so potent is her attraction. He will avert his eyes to shield them both from sin. If somehow forced to shake hands with a woman, he will graze her fingertips with his own, and he flees from the haughty Daughters of Zion who walk with outstretched necks.

For a large segment of modern sabras, the relative monogamy of ancient Israel is back in style, and this time the wife is as relatively free as her husband. It would be nonsense to suggest that this phenomenon is a hearkening back to the ancient days; rather, it is the modern European temper. It must never be forgotten that our sabras are mostly children of firebrands from Russia and Poland, who brought with them to Palestine the bold notions of the 1920's. The German refugees who fled Hitler in the 1930's came to our shores with an attitude toward love and sex best depicted in the savagely cynical drawings of George Grosz. The frank, hard-boiled, and *kaput* views of Hungarian and Roumanian women were also woven into the Israeli pattern. And besides all this, it must be remarked that the parents of our sabras were usually "bohemians"; there was definitely a bohemian stamp to the early Zionist settlers, a carefree, raffish, idealistic, young-hearted tinge that remains. This is confirmed in the often heard quip in Israel. "You've got to be a little crazy to come to this country."

The sabras grew up with this spirit in the air. Every household argued over the experiments of the far-out kibbutzim, who tried out mixed showers—together with vows of chastity—

for their adolescents. In the 1930's a famous Tel Aviv actress calmly had a love child, without benefit of rabbi. The whole country loved her for it, and praised her courage. One must contrast this with the hypocritical banishment of Ingrid Bergman by Hollywood's sex factories in the 1950's.

The sabra, with his passion for honesty and directness, has examined the sometimes giddy ways of his elders, and has retained what he likes of them. The marriage ceremony is a must today, but on the other hand, we have never heard of a sabra girl becoming hysterical, or starting to pack, upon learning that her husband was having an affair.

Life is faced with sabra frankness and contempt for hypocrisy. A mistress is not a future wife; she is a woman who rounds out your life. And life is hard, and short; and passionate love doesn't last. We intend to stay married, because it's good to be married, but why should we be shackled to each other? Why lie and hide at the awakening of new desire? Why not be honest?

Let us begin this controversial subject by hastening to record that many sabras do not live this way at all. As all over the world, there are solid, respectable citizens in Israel who would not dream of straying from the conjugal couch. Among many of our young, whose parents came from such lands as Yeman and Iraq, a wife will often still go with her husband and live with his parents, under the relentlessly watchful eye of her mother-in-law, as has been the wise custom for uncounted centuries. In Jerusalem, there are still pitched battles because men and women (chastely dressed) wish to bathe together at a swimming pool. Ultraorthodox young brides throughout Israel behold their parents' choice of a husband only under the marriage canopy. Many young sabras, whose parents came from North Africa, still make a sign against the Evil Eye, have ten pregnancies before they are worn-out drudges at thirty, go to work every day as a charwoman "sponga lady," and adultery is the last thing on their minds. Besides, they know that such an act would be swiftly revenged with a knife.

But these are enclaves, subcultures that are largely disappearing. One striking example of inevitable change, even among non-Jews in Israel, was told to us recently by the Druse painter Ovadia Elkara. The Druse are a tough, extremely likable religious sect (not Jewish) whose people are mostly scattered through Syria, Lebanon, and Israel. Those within our borders consider themselves loyal Israelis, and hate the Arabs because of centuries of persecution at their hands.

Last summer, an unmarried Druse girl of seventeen became pregnant. In the ancient custom of much of this part of the world, the family assigned her eldest brother to murder her and cleanse the family honor. The young man ordered the wretched girl to walk with him into the fields. They trudged in silence until they reached a lonely spot. The brother stood there, unable to move, and at last his sister cried out passionately, "Why don't you kill me and get it over with? I know that's why you brought me here."

With a sob, the brother embraced his sister and confessed that he was unable to go through with it. It was silly, anyway. They returned home hand in hand, to face the wrath of the family.

Ovadia reports this with awe: the first case of a breach in the fierce tradition. Thus the old order changeth in the old-new land.

But in Tel Aviv and Haifa, the modern Sodom and Gomorrah, many a young girl sabra will not hesitate to dine in any restaurant with a male friend, who may or may not be her lover. A married man will not be afraid to be seen at Haichal Hatarbut, the concert hall around which much of Tel Aviv's social life revolves, with a woman other than his wife.

Of course, many husbands fervently wish that they could conduct their romances in privacy, and think longingly of the anonymous pleasures offered by Paris and New York. But Israel does not offer the gift of privacy. The country is too small. You carry on your affair in a goldfish bowl, aware that your comings and goings are observed with interest. If you head for a weekend at a small pension in Mount Carmel, there are good chances of coming down to the dining room and meeting your dentist, or the man who sold you that car, or your wife's dressmaker.

Separate vacations for husband and wife, among much of our society, are an old Israeli custom. Shocked American visitors tell us that this abomination is against holy matrimony, and worse, against the equally holy idea, for Americans, of "togetherness."

But togetherness is precisely what the hard-working, hard-living Israeli couple want to get away from once in a while. Most of our women work. The long hot summer—seven months without rain—is exhausting. We have only one day of rest a week, not two. Most people live in small, over-crowded apartments. Air conditioning in private homes is still unusual. Windows are flung wide open for the greater part of the year, and the first thing you see in the morning when you step out onto your bit of balcony is your neighbor across the way, in his undershirt. Honking taxis, blaring radios, and budding pianists can drive you frantic. You ride to work in a stifling bus, pressed against sticky flesh. If you live on a kibbutz, you generally eat together with all your comrades, and are together with others almost always. You long to be alone, *just for a while*. (Lack of privacy is the chief reason why women leave kibbutz life and flee to a city apartment.)

By the time your annual two weeks' vacation rolls around, at the height of the blazing heat in July or August, you've had it. You want to get away from everything, husband or wife included. You love him dearly, of course, but you long to see new faces, new scenes, and to find your own identity once more. And if one goes to Eilat or to Galilee and meets a charming man who is also escaping for two weeks, you trade snapshots of the families, and go swimming together in the marvelous bay, and then perhaps you touch, and return home refreshed and eager to get back to the familiar routine.

*   *   *

Yet our private lives, legally, are dominated by Rabbis and medieval scholastics. And nothing has caused more fury in Israel than the imposition of rabbinical rule over what we do within our own homes. (Unlike America, where several protestant varieties of Judaism coexist, Israel has only Orthodoxy.) Less than a third of the population is actively religious and willingly submissive to clerical edicts as to what one may eat, or whom one can marry. The rest of us may have spiritual beliefs, but wish devoutly to be left alone.

But we are not left alone. Despite socialistic parties in political control, our private life in Israel is "ruled" by narrow clericalism to a degree unheard of in any other land in the twentieth century. In Israel, if your name is Cohen, your ancestors were an ancient priestly cast who served in the Temple, and you cannot marry a divorcee. Your wife must be pure. There was an uproar a couple of years ago when a respected judge named Cohen had to fly to America to obtain a marriage ceremony with a woman who happened to be a divorcee. And a rabbi will not marry a Jew to a Gentile, unless the non-Jewish partner embraces Judaism, a drawn-out business. The common practice, if an Israeli wishes to marry a Gentile, is to fly to nearby Cyprus for the weekend, get married, and be back to work on Sunday morning.

The most wretchedness is caused by the nightmare surrounding divorces. Unless divorce is obtained by a rabbi, the older marriage still holds, and any new marriage by any partner is considered null and void. The children born of such a new marriage are born in adultery and are considered as bastards.

If her husband refuses his consent, a woman in modern Israel can obtain a divorce only after years of petitions, hearings, and anguish. A wife cannot divorce a man legally judged insane; the validity of his consent is dubious.

Matters are a little better than they were three thousand years ago, when there was no such thing as an *isha* divorcing her *ba'al*. (In biblical days a woman remained a minor all her life; also, a widow was not allowed to inherit from her *ba'al* unless there were no male heirs.) Today, after years of trying, a wife *may* get a divorce, if she can prove, with male witnesses, that her *ba'al* beats her viciously and constantly. Merely being roughed up once or twice is shrugged off as understandable male pique, or moodiness. If the man promises to behave in the future, the parties are sent home. A wife cannot divorce her husband for any heinous act against her, if he claims to be repentant and anxious to walk in the path of righteousness.

To put it kindly, the Jewish religion by which we legally live favors the male. In biblical days, a *ba'al*, if he wished to repudiate his wife, simply packed her home to her father with some financial compensation. Today, a man obtains a divorce with little difficulty, even without his wife's consent, if he has any reasonable grounds such as her barrenness. A woman who is separated from her husband and suing for divorce does not even dare to receive another man in her home. Her vengeful spouse can instantly claim that she's divorcing him not for drunkenness or for nonsupport, but simply because she wants another man—and that is the end of her chances.

Blackmail on the part of husbands whose estranged wives wish to remarry is not uncommon. We know of several cases where a wife, yearning to be free, bought off her husband with a few thousand pounds, or the gift of their hard-to-get apartment. Tense relations between such once-happy couples are better not described.

*   *   *

The appalled reader may ask; Why on earth do we put up with it? How can less than 25 per cent of the population maintain such an iron grip on the personal life of the majority, which includes avid socialists?

As with everything else in Israel, this requires some explaining of *politika*. The Knesset, Israel's Parliament, is made up of small to fairly large factions representing every shade of opinion in the country. (There was once even a Landlord's party, to fight rent control.) To obtain a clear majority, and run to the country, you have to form a coalition with another party.

Here enter the rabbis. The pious are banded into three religious parties in the Knesset, and receive together some 15 per cent of the votes. This 15 per cent can be crucial; if your party has, say, 40 per cent of the votes, and you make a deal with the rabbis, you have 55 per cent of the votes—and a coalition government is formed.

This system of odd bedfellows is what we have been living under since the state was formed. Even then, violent differences arose in the wording of Israel's Declaration of Independence; the religious wanted God quoted as legitimating the state; the freethinkers objected and they settled for the phrase "The Rock of Israel" has delivered us, etc., and you can decide for yourself, according to your bias, just what was the Rock of Israel.

As a result, there has been at least one member of the

religious parties in every Israeli cabinet. The rabbinical forces could not care less how their coalition partners deal with America, Russia, Arab animosity, labor unions—all that is Caesar's. But the minister of welfare is intensely concerned with preserving Jewishness and the ordained ways of Abraham, Isaac, and Jacob concerning births, marriages, divorces, burials, food, and traffic on the Sabbath. Thus, all questions of personal jurisdiction—marriage, divorce, the sanctity of the Sabbath, etc.—have been vested by the Knesset, by law, in the Rabbinate. This grants them full power in domestic matters over our entire explosive population.

Yet Israel is far from a theocracy, as many outside observers are led to believe when they read of cars being stoned in Jerusalem for desecrating the Sabbath, and many other deplorable incidents. The laws are indeed on the books, but are devoutly broken by many people with a determination that reaches comic-opera proportions. Buses are forbidden on the Sabbath, but you can get to the beach on your one day of rest by riding in a taxi-minibus, which technically runs to carry the stricken to hospitals. Butchers make fortunes by selling black-market pork and bacon (usually raised by an enthusiastically atheist kibbutz), which is kept well hidden in a back room, taken out of its bloody paper wrapping only upon the approach of a customer, then sold as quickly and as feverishly as drugs changing hands in Marseilles, with an eye out for the zealous rabbinical inspectors who pounce down from time to time.

Thus we live. A nation of Jewish rebels, hotheads, free-thinkers—as well as the deeply religious—and we are all ostensibly ruled in our private lives by a minority who live by the Talmud, and who accept every word of the Hebrew Bible as divinely inspired. It is a never-never land of passionate socialists under clerical sway. We are infringed upon by the edicts of medieval rabbis and cabalists who spent their lives commenting on each other's commentaries of the Law, and who devised the 613 precepts by which a Jew must live to become pure before God.

And yet we do not despise the rabbis. We submit to their holy blackmail. Even an Israeli who votes Communist feels a sneaking admiration for the stubborn ritual, the mystic cant, that held Jews together for two thousand years. These fierce-eyed zealots, who throughout history went to the stake praising God rather than renounce their Judaism—What would we have been without them? What kept us together, if not fierce religion? The rabbis live in holy blindness—very well. What meaning has Judaism since Hitler wiped out the *shtetls,* and the synagogues of the Western world became little more than glorified community centers, and more and more third-generation Jews in America intermarry?

Paradoxically, we are sentimental toward the rabbis' holy blindness, although we dislike their meddling in our lives. There is a beautiful old Jewish legend that when after the intolerable long siege, the Legions of Titus set fire to the Temple, the priests flung the keys of Jerusalem high into the air and cried to God: "Stretch out Thy hand, for Thou art now the guardian of these keys!" And in the midst of the roaring flames, a hand was stretching down from the sky; its fingers snatched the keys from the flames and took them.

In 1948, when the Arab Legion of Jordan began its attack on the Jews in the Old City, the rumor spread among the old men that the ancient keys had been found by the Jewish commander of Haganah, the underground army, in the courtyard of the Hurva Synagogue. In 1967, when the Israeli Army actually took the Old City, and the Wall of the Temple was restored to Jewish hands once more, the rumor spread again that the Lord, rather annoyed with the Jews for the last two thousand years, has indeed handed back the ancient keys to Jerusalem.

This is a faith in miracles, and the sabra has lived through many miracles, beginning with the birth of his state. He has been handed back the keys to Jerusalem; he has added a chapter to the Old Testament. It is a mystique of a special Jewish destiny, and the sense of continuum from Moses until today. For the rebellious sabra, the courageous, unwavering, maddening rabbis are the link, the very symbol of what he admires most in that curious stiff-necked people, the Jews.

CHAPTER XII

Kibbutz, and How Not to Be a Jewish Mother

✡ "I have never seen an entire generation so unlike its own parents."
                    —Bruno Bettelheim, *Children of the Dream*

   "My Alex is suddenly such a bad eater I have to stand over him
   with a knife."
                    —Philip Roth, *Portnoy's Complaint*

The main goal of the early utopians to Palestine was to scrap
the old Jew and to invent a New Jew. The first totem they
jubilantly tossed overboard was that revered figure, that
archtype of maternal love and stifling devotion, the all-em-
bracing, all-sacrificing, all-suffering Jewish mother.

   The authority of the father was also exploded, as well as
the idea of the sanctity of the family. As a result of this unheard-of doctrine, and of their revolutionary method of communal child-rearing, the kibbutzim of Israel have produced
two generations of children remarkably free of juvenile delinquency, drug addiction, alcoholism, Oedipus complexes,
homosexuality, sexual malaise, school dropouts, and all the
afflictions of young people today who find life unbearably
meaningless and absurd.

Instead, despite the inevitable clashes brought on by the Big Change, and by frustrated sons of heroic fathers, the kibbutz system has largely produced people who are emotionally secure, anchored to their society, and reasonably content with their lives. As we have stressed repeatedly, the kibbutzim are a tiny minority in Israel, but their ideals have influenced all of us. The make-up of the sabra has been profoundly colored by the kibbutz ideology, which esteems group living and group interdependency above all other relationships. Today, one cannot say that the conceptions of the kibbutzim sway the attitudes of young persons in Tel Aviv and the other cities, but for some forty years the kibbutzim were the social trailblazers. Very many of Israel's leading sabras today were reared in the kibbutz communal nurseries, and others absorbed the attitudes behind it all, even if they were brought up in the customary manner. There can be no real understanding of the sabra without a close look at that extraordinary, radical experiment, the communal Children's Houses of Israel's kibbutzim.

Our first kibbutzniks were young Jewish *intelligentsia* turned peasants (you couldn't get a real peasant to try to farm in the desert, and besides, there weren't any Jewish ones), and their heads were stuffed with Herzl, Marx, Tolstoy, Rousseau, the Bible, A. D. Gordon, and Freud all rolled in one bag of purity. They were extreme left, and ascetics.

With the fervor of new missionaries in the jungle they drained the pest swamps, standing up to their ankles in the buzzing muck, and argued excitedly about The Biological Tragedy of Woman. With the implacable dogmatism of Jewish Jesuits they vowed that *their* women would not be doomed to a dreary life of childbearing and child raising. They dedicated themselves, in capitals, to the Emancipation of the Woman from the Yoke of Domestic Service. The New Jewish Woman would have time to work and to develop her cultural, artistic, and political ambitions.

They toiled like slaves under the merciless sun, men and women alike, and felt sorry for the weak, fearful, unmanly Jew in the Diaspora, in Exile. They were rebels in violent conflict with their own parents back in the ghetto. Gone for good, at least in Palestine, was the strict father figure, and his mate, the overpossessive Jewish mother.

It is worth examining her for a moment. Today in America she is something of a figure of fun, because her anxious, protective traits are superfluous in a land that is kind to Jews. But in eastern Europe she had every reason to be overly concerned with the fate and well-being of her brood.

Like the Italians, whom the Jews resemble in many ways, the Jewish family was all. The mother was the warm, nourishing core of daily life. Barzini speaks of the Italian family as "a sacred ark . . . a refuge, a ship sailing over dark and treacherous waters infested by invisible enemies." With the Jews, the enemies were anti-Semites, and were visible everywhere. Besides, Jews had no country, no nation, no real society. Life was made up of apprehensive peace between one pogrom and the inevitable next pogrom. Jews were accursed, hunted, shunted into ghettos.

But the ghetto was not only a prison, it was a cozy nest, in which *die mama* blessed the Sabbath lights while the winds of hatred howled outside. It was a sanctuary from the cruelties and indignities of the world outside. The father was an awesome symbol of authority, with his fierce eye, his long frock coat which he wore all year around. His word was law, and his cowering, subjugated children would not dream of disobeying him. He was also the captain, who shielded his family as best he could in the violent, hostile land. After a pogrom, he led them to safety to another town, across another river, where the clan would be received by a brother, or a cousin who had managed to find a corner where Jews would be safe for a while.

Despite her commanding husband, and the lowly place assigned to her in Jewish religious custom, the mother was usually the boss of the house. The prize catch for a young bride in the ghetto was a pale, ascetic scholar. He studied the Divine Law, while his wife kept a stall at the marketplace, haggled over soupbones at the butcher's, and boasted that her husband, who spent his days at the synagogue, "didn't know one coin from another." The mother of the ghetto was illiterate, stridently energetic, and it was often she who kept the brood alive, and her children knew it.

Millions of Jews streamed to America at the turn of the century. The winds of hatred were not howling along the streets of New York, and fathers were tailors and tradesmen rather than religious scholars, but the immigrant mothers, and later some of their daughters, clung to their atavistic traits. There was no longer any good reason to overfeed their children because of insecurity, or to overguard them against the next pogrom by drunken Cossacks, but they went right on overfeeding and guarding. They became more and more querulous as they did so, sensing that their role of defender of the brood against catastrophe had ceased to be a valid one.

But the girls who went to Palestine broke loose. If there was one thing they were *not* going to do, it was run a shop, raise a dozen children, and dutifully attend a master-*baal*. The girls also rejected the idea of arranged marriages. That time-honored Jewish custom was unhesitatingly obeyed in the ghetto, or the girls were outcasts and daughters no more.

But in Palestine, almost no one got married on the kibbutzim in the old days, and often not in town, either. It was against their principles. They did not need a rabbi and official documents to tell them it was truly love they felt for their *chaver*, their comrade. A union between a man and a woman was their own affair, to be based solely upon love, and to be broken upon the termination of love. Neither the union nor the breakup required the sanction of the community.

They rather looked down on sex. They were out to conquer sex the way they were conquering the desert. After all, Marx and Lenin abhorred everything associated with the excesses of the flesh. Asceticism was the hard steel of their fanatics' armor, self-denial was the core of their pioneering zeal.

Contrary to all the nonsense written about promiscuity among the kibbutz settlers, they were really puritans. The harsh morality of the biblical prophets had seeped into their bones together with the prophets' fierce love of Zion. Drinking and mild flirtations and promiscuity were frowned upon—and still are.*

In their ruthlessly honest search for truth, some of the early kibbutzim even experimented unofficially with polyandry and polygamy. They were really ready "to begin from the beginning," to grapple with every libido problem, to consider every scheme of sexual behavior that would put an end to neurosis, frustrations, and unhappiness.

Sigmund Freud had just lifted the rock of the conscious mind, and the whole world was staring with fascination at the little insects of the subconscious that were suddenly revealed scurrying beneath it. In the harsh sunlight of Palestine, the New Jews were confident, all bugs would be swept away.

They were naked moralists, and rather smug about it all. They had more important things to think about than fancy clothes, flirtatious dancing, wine—the whole baggage of sexual

* Casual lovers do not ask to be assigned to a common room in a kibbutz, and if they did their request would be turned down with strong disapproval.

trickery.* They were an elite; they were better than everyone else.

If a kibbutz girl was deeply in love, and wanted to "make a life" with her friend, she acquired a *chaver*, a comrade, rather than a master, and the boy acquired a *chavera*, rather than an *isha*, a mere woman. If you knew in your heart that the two of you were a *zug*, a couple, you asked the secretary of the kibbutz to allow you to share a room together. If love ended, alas, you walked out of the room and went back to the bachelor quarters.

The kibbutz was built on the concept of mutual economic security. A *chaver* does not work to support his family, but rather to support the kibbutz. The woman herself is a comrade of the kibbutz; she lives with the man she wants to make her life with, but does not fear the loss of a husband-provider for herself and for her children. In the eyes of the kibbutz, her legal status is not that of a wife, but rather that of a member of the communal society, coequal in all respects with her husband. And most important, though living in the same room with him she is distinct from her partner, not only legally, but as a *human* being. She is not a bourgeoise Mrs. X, with the reflected status of her husband; she has to earn prestige in her own right.

If the love union of the *chaver* and *chavera* did not quite work out, it was believed there would be no tragedy and no shattered lives. They were mature comrades in a kibbutz society. Both were free again without bitterness; there were none of the bourgeois squalid fights over property. The kibbutz, of course, owned all property.

And then the first babies came, and no one knew what to do with them.

*　　　　　*　　　　　*

* Even today puritanism strongly tinges life on a kibbutz; one rarely hears bantering sexual references in mixed company, and among males alone the dirty joke is unknown.

The early kibbutzniks frankly admitted that they did not particularly want children. They feared that their comradeship would be less steadfast with children cluttering up the place. A girl comrade, mother or no mother, should receive her deepest emotional rewards not from her brood, but from the group. Still, she had to be safeguarded from the temptation to revert to a Jewish mother. What to do? How to arrange matters so that their offspring would be free of the detested parental bondage they themselves had endured? How to guard the mother's precious freedom to work, and prevent her from backsliding into the old life of diapers and feedings?

The solution was clear. If the kibbutz idea was good for grown-ups, it was probably good for children. They would organize the children's lives in a miniature kibbutz within the larger kibbutz. It would be a group of children freed from parental commands, a young society of absolute equality with each child subject to his chums' norms and approval, just as the comrades were themselves.

The children would live, play, eat, and sleep away, in their own quarters, quite separated from their parents. The adults would continue to live their presumably rich, full lives; their offsprings would have a golden chance to develop without the defiance, conflict, and anxiety that wracked young lives in a bourgeois society, without being bent or warped by mama's and papa's demands.

In sum, parents and children would keep out of each other's hair. Who knows, the comrades wondered nervously, maybe it would work. At least parents would no longer be The Enemy. They might even find an answer against old Papa Oedipus. They knew it seemed contrary to nature, against all instinct, but they were so bitterly opposed to patriarchal authority and maternal smothering, it seemed a fine idea to remove the child from the parents' clutches entirely.

In a classic book, *A House by the Jordan,* Joseph Baratz,

one of the original settlers of the first kibbutz, Deganiah, wrote, "We were even afraid to marry, because we feared that the advent of children would detach the family from the group." When a child was born to a *chavera* of Deganiah, they were all thunderstruck. The New Jews had been far too absorbed with themselves to think of new New Jews. Did this mean the end of the dream, would their proud girls slide back to the traditional role of Jewish mothers? Not the girls of Deganiah. They were ready to feed the cows, but not their babies. "They wouldn't hear of giving up their share of communal work and life." Besides, none of them had the faintest idea how to look after children.

Some comrades proposed they hire a nursemaid. Dvorah Dayan (the mother of Moshe Dayan) insisted that it had to be someone from "outside," because "so few of the girl comrades knew Hebrew and a child of Deganiah had to be a Hebrew-speaking child." Finally, they chose one chavera whose job it would be to look after the babies as they appeared. They chose a house where the children would be while the mothers worked in the fields. As time went on, the childrens' quarters became a permanent fixture of all the kibbutzim. In almost all of them (but not in Deganiah itself) a newborn infant is taken from its mother some four days after birth, lives together with other children in its age group until he is eighteen, and departs for army service (where he again lives with others his own age).

When does the child see its parents? Between four and six in the afternoon, which is "family playtime" on the kibbutz; and then at bedtime. Also on weekends, holidays, and at spare moments during the day, if it does not disturb the routine of the children or the parents.

Thus was born, quite accidentally, quite pragmatically, the junior utopia that has proved to be the most striking and most famous aspect of kibbutz life. Sixty years have passed since the first scheme of communal child rearing was hit upon at Deganiah, and it is a firmly entrenched method, which the kibbutzim would not dream of abandoning.

Every summer, bemused educators from all over the world flock to Israel's "Other Society" to observe these almost disgustingly healthy children who have been "deprived" of a mother's love and a father's careful care. The famous psychologist Dr. Bruno Bettelheim has examined the "Children of the Dream," and written a first-rate, generally approving book about the sabras of the kibbutz. This, in the academic world, is imprimatur, akin to the Pope's blessing.

*   *   *

Once having hit upon the notion of cummunal childrearing, the kibbutzniks fell to it with zeal. Arguments raged. It was terribly exciting. After all, parenthood, the most responsible task in life, should not be left in the hands of bungling amateurs. Who would take care of the children? Would it really be possible to raise them without their clinging to their mothers? We can't just let them grow, we can't let just clods of nursemaids look after them. Or can we?

The plan that was decided upon was to use permanently assigned women called *metapelet,* and plurally, *metaplot,* to look after the children in the various Children's Houses. There is no English equivalent for metaplot, the closest suggestion would be nurse-helpers, or kindergarten workers. These women, working in teams, run the Children's Houses and make all decisions regarding what goes on there, subject to approval by the kibbutz. The *metapelet* will order a change of diet for a child, not its mother. A doting mother, who hangs around too much at bedtime, will be ordered firmly out by the metapelet on duty. An anxious mother who does not like the toilet training or other discipline her Moshe is receiving from his *metapelet* will have to take the matter up with the kibbutz's education committee.

Somewhere between the age of one and a half and four, depending on the leanings of the kibbutz, the baby is moved to the Toddlers' House. Later, together with a half dozen of his chums, he is a member of the Older Children's House. At fourteen he goes to the regional high school, and boards there. Upon graduation he does his army service. Upon return to civilian life, he may apply to be accepted as a full-fledged member of the kibbutz. Some 90 per cent of the children of the kibbutz *do* wish to live as adults there; they marry, produce their own children, and then the whole cycle begins again, when four days after birth the new baby sabra is enrolled in the Infants' House.

*   *   *

The question that now loomed was: If a child is denied his parent's care, how will he grow? Will he become strongly attached to one of the *metaplot,* regard her as a foster mother? Will he grow up emotionally confused and unhappy? Or what?

Time revealed an intriguing fact. The youngsters were not particularly attached to their *metaplot* (and often disliked them), but they were amazingly attached to each other. In sociologese, the peer group provided the child with ample, satisfying emotional life and growth. He receives an enormous sense of self-reliance from his young mates with whom he lives. He is never alone. He is always in contact with others, receiving stimuli. Significantly, he no longer clings helplessly to a devouring relationship with Mother.

Constantly with his friends, and overseen by teams of *metaplot,* he is not devastated by "separation anxiety and loss" when deprived of the presence of one particular person. He quickly learns to fend and knock about for himself, with the help of older toddlers. Their approval and disapproval guide him in his toilet training, how to sit at the table, how to play, and so on. He wants the approval of his chums, more than the approval of his parents.

The children of the kibbutz become, as Bettelheim and others have observed, remarkably much like twins. They are very close, and have deep dependence and reliance upon each other. They really relax only with another of the peer group. The kibbutz children are not frenzied competitors with each other; they are comrades. There is no urge to compete for parental attention, because the parents are very much in the background, by Western standards. For the same reason, sibling rivalry is muted. There is far less pressure on the child to "achieve." Physical fighting between children is very rare—for one thing, the group is guided to disapprove of fighting, and besides, there are no private possessions to fight over. All property "is ours together," and belongs to the kibbutz.

Indeed, the child is taught to regard himself, and does regard himself, as a "child of the kibbutz." The commune gives him the stability and physical security he needs. He soon grasps that his father and mother are shorn of responsibility for his welfare. The kibbutz storehouse provides his clothes; he eats in the children's dormitory of the kibbutz; the kibbutz nurse or doctor attends him when he is ill. When he is older, he is aware that it is the kibbutz, by vote, that will decide whether or not to take much-needed funds and send him to the University. It will also advise him which profession to choose that would be best suited for the needs of the kibbutz.

In sum, the kibbutz itself and the child's peer group are the strongest formative influences in his life, with his parents running third.

How fare the parents, away from their little ones? Most

will declare that they are all for the system, although a few mothers are unhappy, want to raise their own children. In such cases, the family leaves the kibbutz. Among those who support the system, a certain sense of guilt is probably unconsciously present, for "not being a real mother," as their own mothers were. (This does not apply to kibbutz-reared young sabra mothers themselves, who simply do not feel expected to give more of themselves, because they never got more when *they* were children.) This guilt is also suggested in the remark invariably heard on a kibbutz, "nothing is too good for our children"; and indeed, most kibbutzniks lived for years in tents or shacks, while providing handsome quarters for the Children's Houses.

The evils of most Western parent-child relationships are unknown. There is little hostility or ambivalence. There are no threats of violence from a father, and spankings by parents are just about unheard of. Parents, in a sense, are older, trusted friends, and must *earn* the child's love and respect. In the event of the parents' estrangement or divorce, there is little emotional upheaval and lacerating scars on the part of the child; he goes on living as before. His ties are woven with the peer group. Both parents will continue to visit him during the afternoon playtime, and he will perhaps spend his weekends with his father and mother in turn.

There is, of course, a dark side to this idyllic picture. If a child, because of illness or another reason, has to spend a day or two in his parent's quarters, it is a delightful holiday, but by the third day the strain is apparent and the child is longing to be back with his group. His parents are sometimes guiltily relieved to have him go. By the time the child reaches high-school age parents often complain that "we seldom see our children now; and when we do, we seem to have little in common."

Children grow up far freer of emotional bruises, but they

often also become "emotionally flattened." They are semi-detached, and cool in their relations toward others. As far fewer demands have been made upon them emotionally, they give far less of their emotions themselves. If they *do* feel a lack of love and attention from their parents, this feeling is firmly suppressed. The relaxation of oedipal storms is obvious to anyone who has been close to a kibbutz family; but the price you pay for this is a slackening, a vitiating of all family tensions and ties.

Whether it is worth sacrificing family ties, the love-hate relationship that have made so many of us half-crazy, the reader must decide for himself. The kibbutzniks of Israel are firmly convinced that their admirable and self-reliant young children are proof of the superiority of their system. It should also be remarked that educators have noted that the average kibbutz child is intellectually superior to the average child in America.

*   *   *

Adolescence is not a happy time anywhere; for the kibbutz youngster it is a bewildering time, the cruelest he will know. For his parents, who came to Palestine as teen-agers, it was a joyful never-to-be-forgotten period when they spilled over with energy and threw off their repressions in exultant rebellion against their parents. For the sabra kibbutznik, adolescence is a period when he longs to rebel but absolutely cannot.

In Europe and America, a young person struggles to make his place in life; on the kibbutz, all is designated for him, and there is little personal struggle to win his place. He can, of course, strike out and form a new kibbutz along a dangerous border, but only a small percentage do.

Adolescence is the time of sexual turbulence; the kibbutz sabra is told that sex is a natural joy, but he is firmly expected to keep away from it. Kibbutz youngsters are often tired and listless, and lack the *joie de vivre* their parents had and often still have; many psychologists have ascribed this to sexual repression.

There is also a disturbing aspect to kibbutz adolescence, one that is passed over in the self-congratulatory kibbutz-movement studies on communal education. But this aspect would have riveted the attention of a George Orwell. We are referring to the omnipotent influence of the youngster's peer group. For a teen-ager, it can be a looming, invisible group-pressure that crushes him ruthlessly into the group mold. And after sixteen years of living with and depending upon his friends, the teen-ager is lost without them. All his emotional security is here with them. The fear of rejection by the group, the *chevra,* is the powerful disciplinary force in his life. If he dreams of revolting, of breaking away, it is well-nigh impossible for him to stand alone. He just has not learned how to be alone against the group.

For example, if he defiantly wishes to go to the University and study English poetry, while the kibbutz refuses to give leave or funds for anything but animal husbandry that year, the *chevra* will make him feel an outcast by their disapproval of his action. He cannot conceive of carrying on his revolt against their disapproval. Kibbutz educators are well aware of this "corrective force" of the *chevra,* but see this not as Orwellian, but as "a positive factor in helping the adolescent to identify with kibbutz values."

If the rebellious teen-ager dreams of escaping to Tel Aviv or Jerusalem, he fears that he will not be able to cope with city life all alone. America, or going abroad, is usually out of the question for him, because of money. And his very long-ing to taste the *decadenti* culture of sexy cinemas and Beatles records and discotheques makes him feel guilty: he has been reared to regard all this as sinful and unworthy of "true kibbutz material."

Hopelessly trapped, the teen-ager sometimes now regards the kibbutz as a closed world of repression. He cannot dress as he pleases, or eat where he pleases, and he just cannot bear the idea of living another night in a house with twenty others whom he has known since birth. His parents are utterly unable to help him, and are orthodox kibbutzniks themselves.

He usually gives in. He listens again to his teachers praise his father's heroic struggle for self-realizaton against bitter odds. He feels that is how a real man lives his life, but he is forbidden, in the kibbutz society, from doing the same. He helplessly accepts the kibbutz dictum: "We have created the ideal society, and all you have to do is live in it honorably." His release from his prison (and sexual prison) comes at eighteen, when he leaves for the Army, and gets a chance to be on his own in the world outside.

We do not suggest that this is the attitude of most teen-agers on a kibbutz. But regardless of the fact that many do adjust comfortably to its way of life, the subtle repressions are nevertheless present. But, the kibbutzniks will tell you in their Jesuit way, "The kibbutz method of child-rearing was not designed to raise rebels, but to raise new, *'positivi'* kibbutz members." It has been highly effective in doing so.

Just how effective is revealed in the make-up of the second generation kibbutz sabras—children of parents who themselves were reared apart from their parents. With them, what was highly speculative and daring has become the normal, comfortable way to live. The kibbutz-reared sabras take it for granted that *their* children sleep in the Children's Houses because that is where they slept as youngsters. They assume that their sons and daughters turn not to them, but to their peer group, for security. They are not dismayed at a less than intense relationship with their children, because they never received more from their own parents.

They are rather impassive and depend on group concensus even more than the first generation of kibbutz sabras did. They do not like to make too much of an emotional thing about their children; a sabra mother will come to the child's house at bedtime, say good night, kiss the child affectionately, and depart without fuss, and without the signs of reluctance, the near-tearful anxiety that a nonsabra kibbutz mother will often display at bedtime.

This, of course, does not mean that kibbutz sabra mothers do not love their children. They simply have no guilt feelings about rearing them separately. They take for granted that one raises children separately, in the care of multiple nurses who are surrogate mothers.

*   *   *

For our study of the first million sabras, there is much to ponder here. There is not a single trait of the sabra which cannot be examined in prototype, as it were, among the children of the kibbutz. In the good old days the altruistic pioneer, the *Halutz,* was the idealized image of nearly everyone in the country. All the immigrants had come to be New Jews, and if fate or preference led them to the cities instead of the land, they still considered themselves to be pioneers, building a new social order.

But the kibbutzniks were the vanguard. They were adulated as the cream of the crop, the salt of the earth. It is not surprising, then, that two generations of sabras, throughout the country, copied kibbutz behavior. A girl in Haifa wanted to be "as good as the boys," and learned not to be soft and seductive, not to waste precious time on her hair and her clothes. A boy in Tel Aviv proudly adopted the kibbutz dress of khaki shorts, open sandals, and floppy hat.

What is more, hundreds of thousands of sabras grew up as members of the Youth Movement, fully intending to become kibbutzniks. If you lived in town, and were sympathetic to the idea of the *Halutz* (the man with the plow and the gun), you encouraged your child to join, when he reached the age of ten. The children met on Friday and Saturday nights in neighborhood clubhouses, donned blue shirts, danced horas, and heard a kibbutz leader expound on the nobility of a life as a *chaver*, a comrade. Summers, the child spent working on a kibbutz together with his friends and usually enjoyed it hugely. All this went on until the age of eighteen or twenty, at which time the young person was expected to strike out for kibbutz life. What happened was that most of them did go so far as the initiate stage, *hachshara*, and then quietly, and rather shamefacedly returned home after a year or two. The traumatic results of youngsters raised to be self-sacrificing ascetics, and who wind up as businessmen or city housewives instead, can well be imagined; the effects on their personalities must be much like that of ex-priests and ex-nuns.

But the point that concerns us here is that the majority of sabras wanted to be just like the kibbutz sabras, the famous product of the kibbutz educational system. One longed to be unneurotic, comradely, and deeply committed. One longed to be spartan, uncomplaining, and brave.

Other traits and norms of the Children's Houses also spread quickly to sabras in town. One hid one's emotions; one was matter-of-fact, stolid. As an Israeli psychiatrist has observed, "our children are ashamed to be ashamed, afraid to be afraid." One was unhesitatingly loyal to one's comrades. This, as a hundred books have noted, was fully displayed by the sabra's unhesitating courage and loyalty to his army unit during the Six Days' War.

The kibbutz children's sense of a collective superego was also embraced. Ties to parents among city children in Israel are stronger than they are on the kibbutz, but they are weaker than family ties in other lands. The *chevra,* one's circle of companions, and the *chevra*'s approval or disapproval count for far more among sabras than among youngsters abroad. Consequently, as we have observed, our sabras are often "semidetached," insular, really comfortable only among their own kind—traits so evident in those social test-tube laboratories: the Children's Houses of the kibbutzim.

We return at last, rather roundabout, to our Jewish mother. By being afraid that they would become Jewish mothers themselves, the Israeli mother inadvertently exploded all Western notions about the sanctity of maternal care. If there was one belief cherished by educators and psychiatrists, it was the doctrine that an infant removed from his parents, particularly his mother, and raised together with other children in an institution, was doomed to warped and disasterous results. But as Bettelheim has concluded: "On this count, kibbutz education is a qualified success, though I doubt that its founders gave it a thought: it has disproved the critics and conformed not at all to their predictions. More important, it has clearly reached its own goal: to creat a radically new personality in a single generation." *

* Bettelheim: *The Children of the Dream.*

CHAPTER XIII

The Sabras' Army:
The Intelligent Use of Violence

✡ "It's quite late in the day to have a baby, at my age. But Danny is seventeen and Nili is fifteen, and they'll be going to the army soon. The way things are, their chances of getting killed are as good as their chances of coming out alive."

—Conversation in a Tel Aviv bus, 1969

"Wherever we stroll there are always three—you and I and the next war."

—Contemporary Israeli Poem

"But where was our army?" cried Yael, our eight-year-old sabra daughter, when we tried to explain to her about Hitler, the camps, the six million dead. We groped to make her comprehend that until quite recently there had been no Israel, no Israeli Army, that once Jews lived only in other people's lands. The story exasperated her. It was unthinkable. She didn't want to hear about it. How could we Jews have allowed such a calamitous and shameful situation to exist?

"Where was our army?" sums up the sabra's quite gentile, quite un-Jewish reliance upon his militia, and the intelligent use of violence, to defend his life, instead of dependence upon faith in God or philosophy to explain his death. For a Jew, this is a profound change, perhaps the most profound.

*　　　　*　　　　*

The sabra's total involvement with his army is unique and quite unlike the army-civilian relationship of any other nation in the world today. An Israeli boy, upon reaching the age of eighteen, does his three years of compulsory army service. Girls do twenty months. But upon completion of this, the sabra has by no means "got the army over with," as have youngsters of other countries who finish their tour and return to peaceful pursuits. Israel is dead broke, and except for a tiny officer corps cannot afford a standing army; the sabra himself, the citizen, is Israel's standing army. Besides, there are only some two and a half million people in this country.

With good reason, therefore, the sabra glumly refers to himself as "a soldier with ten months leave a year—eleven, if it's a quiet year."

The sabra's participation in military matters, in time of emergency, begins at a tender age. For example, in the traumatic weeks before the Six Days' War, when nearly all men had vanished into the army, all children helped to erect air-raid shelters, dug slit trenches, delivered the mail, and clerked in grocery stores.

When the sabra is fourteen and enters the gymnasia, (our equivalent to high school), he joins "Gadna," which is a youth organization, much like the Scouts, and is run by the army. "Gadna" service is entirely voluntary, but just about all youngsters sign up for it. It is the thing to do.

At the age of eighteen, the boy and girl sabra begin their respective terms of *sherut chova*, compulsory service, as matter-of-factly as six-year-olds enter elementary school. One has to be in perilous physical or psychological shape to be excused from one's *sherut chova*. Exceptions are rare, and usually a stigma. There are no exemptions for college students. The one fairly large segment that determinedly avoids army service is the daughters of the so-called "Oriental" Jews, many of whom duck out, ostensibly on religious grounds.

There have been no draft-card burnings whatsoever in Israel. After all, the border flare-ups, before the recent war, were seldom farther from the sabra's home and family than a two- or three-hours' drive.

*   *   *

Upon completion of service, the sabra young man and young woman are transferred to *milluim,* the reserves. The girl remains on *milluim* duty until marriage; the man is eligible for reserve call until the age of forty-nine. He is assigned to a specific unit in the special branch in which he has been trained and knows his comrades and officers in *milluim* intimately. He trains with them, every year, for at least four weeks. When the borders are particularly tense, he can expect to be mobilized for the emergency. And this call-up can last until the flare-up simmers down again, or erupts into open warfare.

If you are a sabra, you learn to plan your life, as best you can, around your month of *milluim*—or your husband's— much as citizens in more tranquil lands build plans around their annual holiday.

"We're getting married in July, instead of June, because Yossi has to go on maneuvers first." "We're holding Rafi's birthday party a month earlier, his father's going." "I already had tickets for the Salzburg Festival, and they changed the damn training schedule for our battalion . . ."

It is remarkable that this strict, disciplined life, so alien to the unruly Israeli nature, is accepted with a minimum of grumbling. The Israelis are a curious people who react almost hysterically to normal everyday problems, but rise superbly to extreme hardships. It points up once more how the undebatable need to survive can change a nation's character.

*   *   *

The regular army is the sabra's show. Second lieutenants in the career army are seldom over twenty, first lieutenants and captains are usually not more than twenty-one or twenty-two, and generals are usually in their late thirties or early forties. General Rabin, Chief of Staff during the Six Days' War, received his appointment when he was forty-one, and was the oldest to have held that office since the state began.

Israel has no West Point or Sandhurst. Every officer rises from the ranks. Some served earlier in the British Army fighting Hitler, and not a few spent time in British jails for fighting the British. Just about all of the army's top command belonged in the pre-state days to one of the underground groups: Haganah, Irgun, or the Stern Group.

The fact that the army is the sabra's show is far more remarkable than it would appear: the Old Guard, the immigrant pioneer generation in Israel, has clung tenaciously to seats of power in every other walk of life. They have been adamant in their refusal to let the sabras take charge at last (although, hopefully, the first sabra prime minister may be in office as these lines are read).

But the army has been recognized, instinctively, as the province of the young. In 1948, Haganah was transformed into the national army, and the sabra General Yigal Yadin (better known abroad as the archeologist of Masada) was given the command of Chief of Staff. Since then, Israel's top brass has been made up almost exclusively of sabras. Sabra tone and sabra life style permeates the army—as much as the army permeates the life of the sabra.

This mystique of "hands off the army," and trust in the sabras to run it, is more remarkable when one recalls that in Israel everyone is sure that he knows more about running the country than does the government. Ben-Gurion's famous remark that he was prime minister of a land of a million prime ministers is shrewdly put. Shopkeepers are convinced they know as much of foreign affairs as does Abba Eban, and taxi drivers criticize Jascha Heifetz's cadenzas. The one area where the opinionated Israelis retire from criticism is the army.

The answer for this is not hard to find: Diplomacy, music, fiance are old, old Jewish skills; the art of war is a new art for Jews, and better left in the hands of New Jews.

*   *   *

The structure of the Israeli army is unique. The world has seen nothing quite like it since the citizen-soldier concept common to the small, freer polities of antiquity and the Renaissance. It is a concept of a do-it-yourself militia, that has been rejected by the peace-loving democracies of modern times. And like everything else in Israel, from the revival of Hebrew to the radical communal child-rearing schemes of the kibbutzim, it was born out of necessity, characterized by improvisation, and flourished inordinately.

In 1948, the new state was faced with a grave problem. The days of the underground Haganah were over, and Israel needed a national army. It was surrounded by enemy states who refused to agree to peace. But Israel could barely raise enough money to feed its population, let alone support a large standing army. Besides, every man was needed by the economy. What to do? How to have your cake and eat it, militarily speaking?

Ben-Gurion, who was then prime minister, handed this headache to the General Saff, who came up with an ingenious and revolutionary four-element scheme: a small regular army, consisting almost entirely of officers; universal conscription for boys and girls of eighteen; the planting of agricultural settlements-fortresses along troublesome borders, instead of clearing the borders of civilians and regarding them as no man's lands; and a citizen army reserve that would be the backbone of the army during war. It was daring; it worked, and it still works.

Actually, this citizen-army concept was a continuation of the *Shomrim,* the watchmen of the early Jewish settlements in the country, and of that eager band, the Haganah itself. As inevitably as Haganah was changed from a high-grade sheriff's posse into a passionately dedicated and disciplined commando unit, the commando unit in turn became, with statehood, a people's army.

The Haganah outlook still prevails; in Israel the army is not an elite, a separate entity, but a wartime integration of the people. The army is prosaic, disastrously poor on parade-ground show and spit and polish, and is geared to improvise upon the next unforeseen emergency—as the sabras are themselves. It is wordlessly accepted that the job has to be done, as much as it is accepted that the country has to be built up, without flags and drum beating.

Margalit Banai recalls joining the Palmach, the striking force of Haganah, in the late 1940's, and being packed off to a kibbutz where the Palmach volunteers lived and trained. The Palmachniks earned their keep on the kibbutz by working part time in the fields. Margalit expected a spine-tingling swearing-in ceremony to initiate her into the romantic underground; instead, she was sent out into the broiling sun to dig carrots.

Much of the Palmach's no-nonsense attitude prevails today. The army is no place for adventurers, or thrill seekers. It is a job that must be done, like picking carrots. The drama, sadly, comes later.

*   *   *

In Tel Aviv, and in Israel's other cities, the first thing you notice when the borders are hot and it looks like full mobilization again is the long queues of people at the bus stops. The reason for this is that the army has yanked almost all the buses off the streets, and the bus drivers are carrying reservists to rendezvous points. As the days grow more tense, the lines of civilians waiting for a bus grow longer. Later, everything on wheels is used as army transport: civilian cars, taxis, trucks, wreckers, tractors, and bulldozers. By law, all vehicles must be registered for mobilization in an emergency. The regulations also provide that if your car is mobilized, you can opt to perform your reserve duty as a driver of your own car. Many sabras do.

When you finish your three-year army service and become a reservist, you are given two secret pieces of information: the code warning that your unit has been called up, and the rendezvous point for your unit. You are alerted when you hear these code words flashed over the radio, or by red notices under your door, or simply by a phone call.

If strict secrecy and surprise are essential, as in the Sinai Campaign of 1956, a unique call-up method is employed. You are waked up at night by a man in a car or on a motorbike, who tells you that you've been called up. He hands you a list of a few other reservists for you yourself to arouse that night and tells you to report before dawn. He says a terse *shalom*, and departs.

You kiss your wife and children good-bye, hunt for and pull the other six chaps out of assorted beds, in the middle of the night, which can be quite an experience in itself. Students drop their books, usually leaving a note pinned on their girl friends' doors: "They've called me. So don't forget to make a carbon copy of your notes on Eisenstadt's lectures."

Workers drop tools, lawyers and engineers try to wind up their affairs. All seems slipshod confusion, but this manpower reserve quickly slips into assigned slots to form a remarkably efficient fighting machine. Fully equipped brigades of reservists are usually at the front within forty-eight to seventy-two hours.

Officers and men wear the same mass-produced uniforms, with insignia the only sign of distinction. Officers eat with noncommissioned officers, but all the food comes from the same kitchen. (In the good old days of the War of Liberation, it was common to see a brigade commander queue up at a field kitchen behind a buck private, and later the general would wash his own mess tin.) There is little saluting; the egalitarian convictions of the kibbutzim and of Israel itself prevail. The atmosphere is jaunty, both strangely tense and informal.

This, then, is the "rabble in arms" that in 1967 fought and won one of the largest tank battles in history. Millions of words have been written about the courage and dazzling efficiency of the Israeli army in battle, and there is no need to praise it here. The high price Israel pays for her army's daring, however, must be pointed out. Eight hundred soldiers fell in the Six Days' War, but this number is comparable to sixty thousand dead in an American army within a single week.

An extraordinary number of these casualties were officers. Israeli officers, for a generation, have been taught not to order "Forward!" but rather the soft-spoken call, "Follow me!" In the savage fighting on the Syrian front in the last war, the Golani Brigade sustained fifty casualties in the conquest of the Syrian heights. Thirty-four were officers.

Integrating East and West into the sabra mold is a tremendously important job of the Israeli Army. The 1.2 million immigrants, who have come in two decades, mostly as refugees from the Muslim lands of Africa and Asia, and are called "the Oriental Jews," or, by those who believe that the "Orientals" are treated shabbily, "the Second Israel," now make up more than half the country's population. Sixty per cent of elementary school children now come from this "Oriental" background. The average fertility rate of Israeli women from "Oriental" lands is 6.1; the rate of women from European backgrounds is 1.9. The proportion of sabras in Israel today is at least 7 to 3 in favor of the "Orientals."

These Jews from such places as Morocco, Algeria, Iran, Iraq, Turkey, Egypt, and Afghanistan are strikingly different from the settlers who arrived from Western countries. They are profoundly "backward," and their ways of life had little to do with the twentieth century. What is more, they arrive in Israel penniless and unskilled, and are therefore at the bottom of Israel's economic ladder. They are the most underemployed group in Israel's society: about one third works for only part of the year. As late as 1961, there were ten thousand young Israelis in Israel's leading colleges and universities; and of this number only five hundred were "Orientals." Today, only 13 per cent of the college enrollment is made up of "Orientals."

All the observations pertaining to "disadvantaged" minorities anywhere in the West apply to the "Orientals," only in Israel they happen to be a majority. And soon they will be an even larger majority; it is expected that within ten years, because of the differences in the birth rate, "Orientals" will make up 80 per cent of Israel's population.

This is a terrific problem because the "Orientals," with their sharply lower income per home than the Westerners, must support far larger families. Israel's school system is not really geared to help them get ahead—as in most other countries, the schools encourage the bright child who already has a familiarity with the subject matter and the cultural norms.

Are things getting better? Most authorities do not think so. Dr. Israel Katz, director for the Hebrew University's

School of Social Work, warned recently, "The gap has in-
creased between these two groups, and is increasing right
now."

Curiously, most Israelis are not worried about all this. The
Western sabras themselves have shown little enthusiasm for
volunteering for work in the poor villages and development
towns where most of the "Orientals" live. The familiar cocky
sabras reply, *"Yeheyeh beseder"*—it will turn out OK—sums
up his attitude. It's only a matter of time until they're in-
tegrated, the sabra feels. We thought it would take ten years,
but we've had a few other problems in the meantime, and it
looks as though it might take twenty.

The "Orientals" themselves, of course, are furious about
this state of affairs. They see most of the top jobs and op-
portunities go to the educated Western Jews, who also have
the comfortable villas. They are torn between the emotions
that the Arabs themselves feel toward the Jews—pride in their
own ancient ways, and jealousy and resentment of the successful Westerners.

Many of the "Orientals" are bitter about Israel, and blame
"the Europeans" for all their troubles. Many would leave
tomorrow for France or America if they could. The sabras
from "Oriental" homes often have ambivelant love-hatred
feelings toward the national image of the sabra, which, after
all, has been that of a westernized sabra.

In Tel Aviv's vast near-slum of Shunat Hatikva, where
thousands of "Orientals" live, life is squalid, and bewildering.
They are caught between East and West. Their dilemma is
much like that of New York's Puerto Rican immigration;
they are people from hot lands where dignity and manly
pride are all, and now they often find their pride and dignity
trampled upon. They look forward to a life of shabby jobs in
shabby homes, although theoretically, as with America's
blacks and browns, the doors are open to all.

What has all this got to do with the Israeli Army? Everything: the army has proved to be the most successful force for integration and education that Israel possesses—far more so than our schools. For one thing the schools are hard-pressed just to keep up with the waves of new immigrants. Besides, in the words of Dr. Judith Shuval, of the Israel Institute of Applied Social Research, "The school system is structured to prevent mobility of under-privileged children through it. It is a system that is geared to an elite . . . It filters out the kids the system should be more interested in helping."

But the army, which depends crucially on the successful teamwork of men flung together from East and West, is vitally interested in helping them to integrate. It compels the recruit lately from Cochin, where one squats on one's haunches and eats out of a common family bowl, to eat and live with Roumanian immigrants and kibbutz sabras.

Illiteracy is no reason for being rejected by the army. If you can not read and write, they will teach you. If you have had no primary school education, you get one. You also learn a vocation; and boys who would never have been able to be more than unskilled hands emerge as mechanics and draftsmen.

Above all, the "Oriental" recruit feels a sense of belonging. He feels cared about, and his pride is carefully enhanced, not broken; the army respects the "Oriental's" pride of manhood and initiative and courage as much as he does himself. If he has the ability to command, he commands. The recruit, in turn, is by the time of his discharge much closer to the "acculturation process of the national image of the sabra."

It works. For some years in Israel there was some apprehension that "the Orientals would dilute the sabra spirit." But in the recent war the "Oriental" sabras fought for their new land just as bravely and as tenaciously as did the Western sabras.

*　　　　*　　　　*

It is all very odd. Much of the young of America despise their Establishment and riot against their military hierarchy. They gag or giggle at ultrapatriotic phrases, and prefer the black humor of *Catch-22.*

But the sabra is a square. He cannot afford the easy internationalist and pacifist leanings of American youth, because he's constantly in danger of being bumped off. He does not despair of his Establishment or find it absurd; he knows that if it goes under, so does he. He believes that it is sweet and fitting to die for one's country.

The sabra's militarism has taken the world's image of the Jew a long, long road since Goethe heard Felix Mendelssohn play the violin, and exclaimed, "What a talented Jew-boy!" The sabra's militarism has also changed the modern Jew's own certain contempt and repugnance for the military reputation. Moses, according to David Ben-Gurion, was the first Jewish general. But Leon Trotsky, who led the Red Army, was one of the few Jews to annotate Clauswitz.

In this chapter we have traced the unique relationship between the sabra and his army. There is another uniquely Israeli institution which, sad to say, has become more and more part of Israeli life. This is called the Bereaved Parents Association.

This group consists of parents who have lost children in Israel's wars, or in the constant border raids, flare-ups, and reprisal actions. They proffer condolences to newly bereaved parents, and to newly created widows and orphans. For example, after the Suez Campaign in 1956, bereaved parents received condolences from parents who had themselves lost sons and daughters in the War of Liberation of 1948. After the Six Days' War of 1967, these same parents tried to console the newly stricken parents whom the new war had embittered, and repeated the same words of comfort they themselves had been told: Let us try to find solace in the independence of Israel.

CHAPTER XIV

The Next Million Sabras

✡ "Happy the nation whose annals of history are boring to read."
—Montesquieu

"When peace comes, when peace comes,
Egyptian football teams will beat us in Tel Aviv,
We shall go by train to Damascus,
We shall go skiing to the Lebanon."
—Pop tune in Israel during the Six Days'
War

It will be a miracle if there are another million sabras. But then, it has been a miracle that the first million appeared, fought off all menaces, and flourished. Will our new breed endure and prosper? Or is it doomed, as Ben-Gurion and others have brooded, to be a brief mutation, a short-lived, gallant episode in the long history of the Jews? Long-range predictions are off limits in the Middle East. But one fact is clear: whether or not the sabra is here to stay depends on his keeping at bay eighty million Arabs who hate his guts.

You can write about the English or the Chinese without once mentioning another people, but you cannot describe the sabra without discussing his *doppelgaenger*, the Arab. The sabra's situation is rather like that of a mountain child born into his family's bitter vendetta with another clan over the same piece of land. So fervid are the passions, and so explosive, they almost sweep aside all other considerations in life.

The sabras are the only people in the world who wake up every morning surrounded by a ring of enemy nations who for more than twenty years have publicly demanded and worked toward their extermination. And Israel, before the Six Days' War, was the only state in the world whose parliament stood less than a mile away from enemy shells and mines. As we have seen, this precarious condition is the sabra's basic fact of existence.

We have no intention of haranguing the reader with the rights and wrongs of the Israel-Arab conflict. This painfully complex subject has been dealt with in a hundred books, and the reader has no doubt formed his own bias concerning it. What interests us here is how the sabra feels about the Arabs, and how they affect his life.

Curiously, the sabra has no hate for the Arab. The wistful pop lyrics at the head of this chapter are in striking contrast to the bloodcurdling songs the Arabs sang just before the Six Days' War. This is no fortuitous pose on the sabra's part; he longs to be accepted not as an invading foreigner, not as "a thorn in the flesh of the East," but as an uprooted ancient people restored to the fabric of the region.

He usually admires Arab-style architecture more than that of his own Tel Aviv. He often sports an Arab-style mustache. He gravitates toward Levantine coffee houses. *Shashlik* and *kabab* are the national dishes of young Israelis (to the dismay of Jewish tourists), not chicken soup and corned beef sandwiches. He loves the open landscape of the East, and works unconcernedly in the searing hot *khamsin* wind, while immigrants droop and flee when it blows. In sum, it is no exaggeration to say that many sabras feel they have more in common with an Arab in Nazareth or the Old City of Jerusalem than they have with a Jew in Hampstead or Miami.

At the same time, he is furious with the Arab leaders for cynically using the wretched Arab refugees as pawns, to appeal for world sympathy. For example, the refugees in the Gaza Strip, under Egyptian control for twenty years, were forbidden to leave the Strip and enter Egypt. He is angry with the world for shrugging off the seven hundred thousand *Jewish* refugees from Arab countries who have been forced to flee their homes since Israel was founded.

Despite all the grave obstacles, the sabra is convinced he can coexist in peace with the Arabs. He often feels that his father might have been less inflexible and more imaginative in dealing with the problem of the Arab refugees. When he is finally given leadership, we believe that his sabra generation will be vigorous and successful on this score.

World politics—the pseudo-Machiavellian scheming of Britain a generation ago, the cynical, sinister Russian fishing in troubled waters today—these have been the enemies of peace in the Middle East. But there is another profound factor, the psychological and emotional clash between Jew and Arab, of which the sabra is far more keenly aware than was his father.*

The sabra know that the Israelis have affronted Arab dignity and pride and manhood. For the Arabs, the Jews were like a ruthlessly honest mirror in whose reflection the Arab beheld his own arrested culture, his failure to succeed in twentieth-century terms. The Jew was hated because he launched a modern, successful Western state in the midst of the Arab's squalor and corruption. Despite Israel's long state of siege, it has remained a genuine democracy, the only one within a radius of a thousand miles.

---

* T. E. Lawrence remains the best teacher on this sad subject. In *Famous Dictum*, Lawrence once wrote, "There are no half-shades among Semitic peoples, they see everything in black and white extremes. . . . These people of spasms, of upheavals, of ideas."

For the pioneer generation, such as Ben-Gurion, the Arabs were one more obstacle to be dealt with, along with hunger, malaria, and British about-faces. For them it was not a moral problem, but rather a political headache that the Palestine promised by the British to the Jews in 1917 was inhabited by the Arabs, and ruled by a third nation, the Turks.

And so the noble adventure began. We will make the desert bloom, the Zionists reasoned; we will raise the standard of living, fight disease and hunger, and the Arabs will be grateful to us. But the Zionists made no determined effort to win over the Arabs, or to blend with Arabic culture. "Unlike other colonists," one observer noted a quarter of a century ago, "the Jews brought no glass beads or rum, but they brought no missionary bibles, either. . . . Palestine was their promised land, doubly promised from Mount Sinai and from Downing Street."

The Zionists would have been astonished to hear that more vigorous cooperation with the Arabs was expected of them (assuming that any Arabs might have welcomed it). Were the Jews not coming with the blessing of the Balfour Declaration to build a Jewish Home? Were they not yearning to run the place virtuously and effectively, for the mutual benefit of Jew and Arab?

But the more "progress" the Jews brought in, the more the Arab world and Arab pride hated their shining example of what could be done in the region if anyone really cared to do it. This, in our opinion, was "the Great Thorn" of the Israel-Arab clash, almost as insoluble as the political factor: Arab resentment and envy of the Jewish accomplishment, compounded by their humiliating defeats in battle with the Jews.

Hatred of the Jews became the Arab leaders' best method of uniting their own nations. The Jewish state was painted as the source of all misery and evil in Egypt and in the other Arab lands. And the fact that the Jews did not much hide that they regarded themselves as members of a superior race, and rather patronized the backward Arabs—all that is summed up in the Israeli pejorative expression *"Arabush"*—did not exactly make things easier.

The cultural gap between the two peoples grew wider from year to year. Jews and Arabs lived their lives in restricted, watertight compartments, as it were. The Zionists, with their dream of a Hebrew nation reborn and daily harassed by crushing problems, including Arab animosity itself, could hardly be expected to find a way toward symbiosis between themselves and the Arabs.

All this, of course, is lofty hindsight. No one can ever say that if the Jews had been less Hebrew-obsessed, less provocatively alien, the story would have been less bloody and less tragic.

In any case, this is the bewildering clash of interests which the sabra has inherited. In his pragmatic way, he argues about it all much less than his father did. He hopes that he can somehow work it out. Meanwhile, he clings to his "small notch"—Lord Balfour's phrase when he commented that Palestine represented less than 1 per cent of the vast areas of Turkish-liberated lands which Britain set up for the Arabs after World War I. (The other 99 per cent of land eventually became Jordan, Iraq, and other states.) The small notch of Palestine, for the sabra, is nonnegotiable.

* * *

It has been the sabra's great misfortune to arrive late—the planet had by then been divided up and there were no more empty spaces. It has also been his great fortune to arrive just in time—ten years later all the new pro-Arab African states had joined the United Nations, and there would not have been the faintest chance of a Jewish state being created by a U.N. vote, as it was in 1947.

Nowhere, until the "peaceful" birth of Israel, does history

contain an example of a state being founded by international consensus. All mankind's history has been a history of invasion, of conquest of people by people, and deportation of populations and their absorption by other nations. Virtually every sovereign state we know has been created by violence and lawless upheaval which the world accepted in time as a *fait accompli*.

But, ironically, the sabra would have been far better off if Israel had not been hatched out by diplomats of the United Nations; if the story had been buried in the back pages of *The New York Times* instead of being front-page headlines for a generation; if the fight between the Jew and Arab had been a minor desert fracas instead of a world-spotlighted drama. In words of Harvard's Nadav Safran, "Had the big powers not imposed their protection . . . peace would have been concluded in 1949, and people would probably be talking today about the national affinity of Semites, instead of their mysterious obstinacy."

Perhaps. But the sabra's fight seems doomed to the world's front pages. He is glumly resigned to the prospect of another twenty years of no-peace. It is a melancholy prospect, but until "Egyptian football teams will beat us in Tel Aviv," the sabra sees no alternative but to go on playing the role of the Indian fighter.

*　　　　*　　　　*

If all goes well, there are other grave headaches the next million sabras must grapple with. The most burning problem, in the sabra's eyes, is how to blast Israel's Old Guard out of their seats of office. In politics, in government departments, in medicine, in business, in industry, the sabras are champing impatiently while white-haired old-timers cling tenaciously to power. An American senator once remarked that Israel is not a democracy but a generocracy. This is hard to believe, but almost true. David Ben-Gurion, Levi Eshkol, and Golda Meir governed Israel while in their seventies. The median age of the Knesset is the highest in the world. Allon and Dayan, in their early fifties, are the "young" members of Israel's twenty-two-member cabinet, as this is written.

"For I never knew so young a body with so old a head," Shakespeare wrote in *The Merchant of Venice,* and this, unhappily, applies only too well to Israel. It is due in great part to the hallowed tradition of "vetek," seniority. You sit in your chair, and the years carry you forward.

"Vetek" also rules in Israel's politics, where voting follows the English party-list system. You do not vote for your favorite man, you vote for a party. This prevents an ambitious, exceptional young man from getting ahead quickly in public life, no matter how popular he may be. There is no proportional representation in Israel, no such thing as a man running for Knesset and wooing the voters and being in the limelight where his merits are studied.

Nevertheless, things are looking up for the sabra. Tourism leaps from year to year, and the hectic economy somehow is booming. Immigration is up again, after dwindling to a perilous low. Despite crushing taxation—Israel now spends twenty times for arms what it did in 1950—there are hopeful signs that for the next million sabras life may be less hard and more pleasant.

In the meantime, the peculiar mixture of the sabra's life goes on. A sabra navy officer, married to a Gentile girl, brings court proceedings to make his life less onerous; and Israel's Supreme Court declines to rule on who is a Jew and who is not—after four thousand years of Jewry, no one is quite sure. Daily, sabras are maimed and killed fighting the Arabs along the borders, and the children of the kibbutzim facing the Golan Heights now sleep nightly in air-conditioned underground bunkers. At the border settlement of Hamadyla, the sabras opened a discotheque named *Katyusha,* after the Soviet-built rocket launcher, whose shells have been hitting the settlement for months.

Although sorely beleaguered, this tiny nation with the largest per capita theater audience in the world offers everything from the classics and the internationally popular Broadway musicals to Breckett, Genet, Ionesco, Sartre, Pinter, Arrabal, Anouilh, DeGhelderode, Arnold Wesker, O'Neill, O'Casey, Synge, Thornton Wilder, Arthur Miller, Tennessee Williams, Albee, Murray Schisgal, Arthur Kopit, Jules Feiffer and LeRoi Jones.

The next million sabras will certainly be more sophisticated than the first. Every year more young Israelis study in universities and do post-graduate work abroad. Israel is a nerve center of the world's growing Uniculture: American, French, and German paperbacks are on sale everywhere, and *The New Statesman, Time* and *Der Spiegel* vie for space in the corner kiosk, along with *Moscow Life* and *Playboy.* Our theater grows less puritanical. Musically, the sabra has the best of everything; internationally, famous artists come yearly to Israel, and there is not a single major phonograph record company in the world, with the exception of one German label, whose products are not pressed locally in Tel Aviv.

The old-timers, the parents, have done more than their share to prepare and to build the New Jerusalem; they do not rush around as much as the young people; they snooze in the heat of the day and gossip with their neighbors in the cool of the evening. It is as though so much has been accomplished during their lifetime, they can afford to sit on their balconies and gaze at what has somehow miraculously grown around them. Their task is done—one can almost feel this in the air as one strolls about Tel Aviv at eight in the evening and gazes up at the breadwinner, home from work, sitting in his undershirt on his open balcony, his evening paper and a glass of fruit juice in his hand, and his radio blaring away.

It is the sabra's turn now. He has inherited Zion, and is at ease in Zion. Will he be "a people dwelling apart," as the ancients called the Jews, or will he become "Like all the other nations," as Herzl predicted? And if he does become the latter, is it "the end of the Jewish people," as George Friedmann and others fear? It is too early to tell. (Besides, prophecy is a dangerous business among the Jews, there is too much competition.)

There is another intriguing question: Will the next million sabras be like the David who beat Goliath or the David who wrote the Psalms? Solomon the Monarch, or Solomon the Philosopher?

It all depends, of course, on whether the sabra is allowed to live in peace. If he is, there is no telling what effect the shock of peace will have on the young Israelis who have been born and raised in war and turmoil. As Herzl wrote, "God would not have kept the Jews alive for so long, unless they still had a special role to play in the history of mankind."

And toward the end of his life, the feeble, blind Dr. Chaim Weizmann told the United Nations Special Commission on Palestine, "God has chosen the small nations as a vessel through which he sends his best messages to the world."

We believe that the sabra, if he can ever put down his gun, has much to contribute to the world. The great archetypes of Jewish history are not the Maccabees and the warriors of Masada, but rather the spiritual leaders, the anxious moralists, the wrathful prophets, the revolutionary thinkers from Moses and Jesus to Marx and Freud.

The Jew was not meant to live by the sword. But, of course, it all depends on whether the sabra is what you call a Jew.

Index